MW00344125

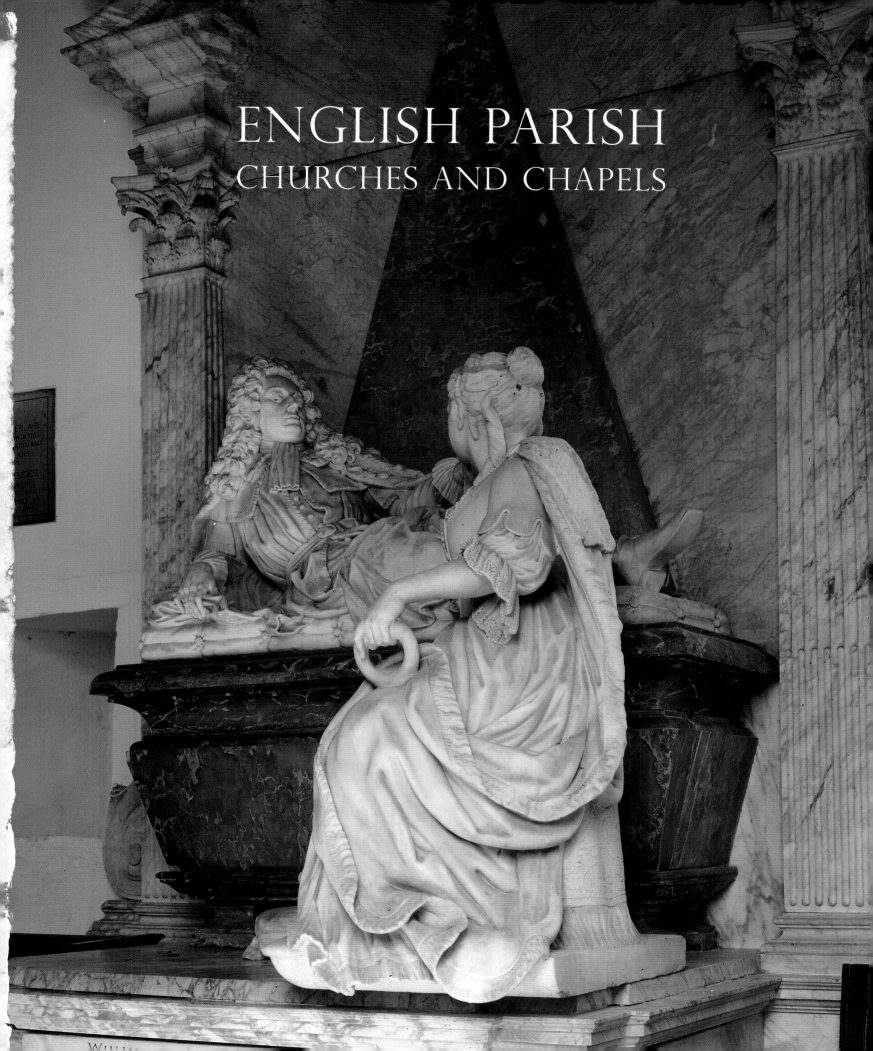

ENGLISH PARISH
CHURCHES AND CHAPELS

SHIRE PUBLICATIONS
Bloomsbury Publishing Plc

PO Box 883, Oxford, OX1 9PL, UK
1385 Broadway, 5th Floor, New York, NY 10018, USA
Email: shire@bloomsbury.com

SHIRE is a trademark of Osprey Publishing, a division of Bloomsbury Publishing Plc

© 2017 Matthew Byrne

First published in Great Britain in 2017 by Shire Publications. Second impression 2020.

All rights reserved. Apart from any fair dealing for the purpose of private study, research, criticism or review, as permitted under the Copyright, Designs and Patents Act, 1988, no part of this publication may be reproduced, stored in a retrieval system, or transmitted in any form or by any means, electronic, electrical, chemical, mechanical, optical, photocopying, recording or otherwise, without the prior written permission of the copyright owner. Enquiries should be addressed to the Publisher.

Every attempt has been made by the Publisher to secure the appropriate permissions for material reproduced in this book. If there has been any oversight we will be happy to rectify the situation and written submission should be made to the Publisher.

A CIP catalogue record for this book is available from the British Library.

Matthew Byrne has asserted his right under the Copyright, Designs and Patents Act, 1988, to be identified as the Author of this Work.

ISBN: 978 1 78442 239 4
PDF ISBN: 978 1 78442 241 7
ePub ISBN: 978 1 78442 240 0

Cartography by www.bounford.com
Typeset in Perpetua and Avenir
Page layout by Myriam Bell Design, UK
Originated by PDQ Digital Media Solutions, UK
Printed and bound in India by Replika Press Private Ltd.

20 21 22 23 24   10 9 8 7 6 5 4 3 2

The Woodland Trust
Shire Publications supports the Woodland Trust, the UK's leading woodland conservation charity.

www.shirebooks.co.uk
To find out more about our authors and books visit our website. Here you will find extracts, author interviews, details of forthcoming events and the option to sign-up for our newsletter.

Half title page: At Drayton Beauchamp church, Buckinghamshire, Lady Newhaven mourns the death of her husband, Lord Newhaven, who died in 1728.

Title page: Fairfield church stands alone on Romney Marsh in Kent.

Contents page: The capital of a fourteenth-century pier at the church of St Peter and St Paul, Dorchester-on-Thames, shows two cowled canons sleeping under an oak tree.

ENGLISH PARISH
CHURCHES AND CHAPELS

Architecture, Art and People

Supported by the National Churches Trust

MATTHEW BYRNE

CONTENTS

AUTHOR'S NOTE

THERE ARE OVER 30,000 CHURCHES and chapels in England. Of these some 16,000 are Anglican parish churches, of which about 10,000 predate the sixteenth-century Reformation. Roman Catholic and Free Church buildings account for the remainder. The National Churches Trust supports all these denominations in the care of their churches and chapels. Since only a minute fraction of such a large number can be described in one book the difficult problem of selection has been based on a number of criteria. The churches and chapels chosen are geographically and historically representative of the total. Thus, all areas of the country but not all counties are included. All the architectural periods and styles are presented, from early Anglo-Saxon to the modern era. In addition to this, the selection includes churches of very different types and character, from grand churches of cathedral size with sumptuous furnishings to churches of more typical size and, last but not least, those small, lovable ones that have escaped Victorian restorations and have retained their rustic character, not just externally but also internally, where the atmosphere is steeped in the spirit of past generations. All the important types of furnishings and works of art from within these buildings have been included in this work.

A book on churches can be created in a number of ways. The best way to enjoy the beauty and the thrill of a particular church is obviously by undertaking a personal visit to see every aspect of its architecture and furnishings and to learn about its history at leisure, preferably with a guide or guidebook. This seemed to provide the best model for a book – one that would take a representative selection as described above and show each building in some detail as a visitor might find it. Although based on this approach only a very small number of churches and chapels could be chosen, it seemed preferable to presenting only fragmentary glimpses of a much larger number.

The enjoyment of a church and its furnishings is of course essentially a visual thing and in a book it can only be enjoyed through the photographs, which are therefore the essence of this volume. However, there are many invisibles behind the visible features that make churches what they are. Churches are meeting places of the divine spirit with human beings, and the buildings in their present forms are the result of changing beliefs and attitudes in several spheres: religious, political, social, emotional and artistic. A knowledge of why, how and when this happened is likely to help in the understanding and enjoyment of what is seen. It is hoped that the text will complement the photographs in this way.

It seemed desirable to have some discernible system when choosing the order in which the selected churches were described. Although this book is in no way intended as a history of English church architecture the chapters are arranged in a broadly chronological order based on the ages of the churches to give the reader some sense of the passage of time over the centuries. Only a few churches belong entirely to any one period as the product of a single building campaign. In their architecture and furnishings most are a complex mixture of a long evolution, and in these cases the most important and interesting features have determined the placing of a church. Each of the chronological sections is preceded by a short summary of the principal features and, most importantly, of the distinctive spirit of the period. Hopefully this has avoided undue repetition in the chapters that follow.

Of course nothing in a book can equate with visiting the real places, and some readers of these guided photographic tours may be encouraged to visit these churches and chapels for themselves or some of the many thousands that cannot be included.

Matthew Byrne
December 2016

ACKNOWLEDGEMENTS

THE MAJORITY OF THE PHOTOGRAPHS in this book, as well as many others, were taken over a period of nearly 40 years. On my visits to each church I was accompanied by a silent guide and indispensable companion. From 1948 to 1974 Professor Sir Nikolaus Pevsner, an eminent architectural historian and indefatigable traveller, toured the English counties in turn inspecting all buildings of architectural significance, including their interiors where appropriate. During these inspections his sharp eyes missed little. Each night the day's notes were written up to be later analysed and interpreted, leading each year to the publication of one or more of the county volumes of his monumental *Buildings of England* series. Since his death these volumes are being updated and enlarged continuously. They are indispensable to everyone interested in ancient or modern architecture, be it an individual building or a whole town or city. They have guided the planning of my excursions and my choice of things to photograph on site as well as greatly informing the text of this book. Unless otherwise stated all direct quotations are from this source. I am also indebted to the informative and well-produced guide books published by so many churches. They have been especially valuable in giving information about local personalities and events connected with the churches. However, I am solely responsible for any factual errors.

Access to churches outside of services is made possible only due to the generosity of many people. Many village churches can be open every day without an attendant. Some of England's greatest architectural and artistic treasures reflecting the history of its people can be seen at close quarters, often in complete solitude. In busy city and town centres, to have the churches open for visitors it is often necessary for members of the congregation to serve in rotas as watchers and guides and to provide a friendly welcome. In remoter areas it is sometimes necessary to keep a village church locked for security reasons. There are people in vicarages, cottages and farmhouses who 'keep the key' and who come to their front doors from kitchens, living rooms and gardens to hand it over with invariable good humour and, when necessary, to give advice on how to manipulate ancient keys in equally ancient locks – in the right door. This lifelong church explorer, and I am sure many others, is grateful to these people who enable English churches to be always accessible to everyone.

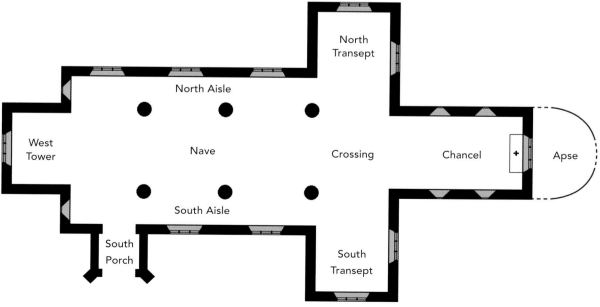

A common ground plan of a major church during all the periods covered by this book. Smaller churches may contain only some of the areas indicated.

IN
AFFECTIONATE REMEMBRANCE OF
WARD HAWKINS CHENEY, C.B.
COLONEL IN THE ARMY
SON OF ROBERT CHENEY Esqr
LANGLEY, DERBYSHIRE. HE WAS BORN 1st Nov. 1778.
AN CORNET THE SCOTS GREYS IN HOLLAND,
OF YORK. HE WAS SEVERAL WOUNDED
THE SAME REGIMENT AT WATERLOO
OUR HORSES WERE KILLED
WOUNDED UNDER HIM) AND HIS COMMAND
THE COMMAND DEVOLVED UPON HIM
ELIZA YOUNGEST DAUGHTER OF
JOHN AYRE ESQ. OF GADDESBY.
AND DIED THERE 3. MARCH 1848.

SACRED
TO THE MEMORY OF
ELIZA, WIFE OF
Colonel EDWARD HAWKINS CHENEY, C.B.
AND DAUGHTER OF THE LATE
JOHN AYRE Esqr OF GADDESBY.
WHO DIED ON THE 16th DAY OF MAY 1818.
AGED 32 YEARS.
"I CRIED UNTO THE LORD GOD IN THE DAY OF MY TROUBLE,
AND HE GAVE EAR TO ME"
ALSO, TO THE MEMORY OF
JOHN AYRE CHENEY, INFANT SON OF THE ABOVE
EDWARD HAWKINS & ELIZA CHENEY
WHO WAS BORN ON THE 21st DAY OF MARCH,
AND DIED, ON THE 30th OF JULY 1818.

EDWARD H. CHENEY, C.B. COLONEL IN THE ARMY LATE SCOTS GREYS.

FOREWORD

By Michael Palin

WHEN I RETURN TO ENGLAND from travelling abroad the most instantly reassuring sight from the aeroplane window is a landscape scattered with churches. Even a small cluster of houses will have a stout stone tower at their centre. Our churches have always taken pride of place in a community, not just for worship but also the practical business of sheltering people from the elements, providing havens for farmers on market days, and marking our lives through births, marriages, and deaths.

The relatively settled social history of our country has ensured not only the longevity of many of our churches but also the evolution of a restrained, dignified and harmonious architectural style. Cathedrals are grand and designed to impress with the might and majesty of God, but by and large parish churches are structures of strong and simple lines rising above the communities they serve in a protective, rather than dominating fashion.

In this rich and detailed book, Matthew Byrne selects a collection of places of worship to prove what potential treasure troves of local – and national – history they represent.

Holy Trinity, Blythburgh, in Suffolk, is a prime example of such historical richness and like so many handsome East Anglian churches, reflects the great wealth that accrued from the woollen industry during the Middle Ages. That industry has long gone, and today Blythburgh church serves only a small village. However, it has been maintained in all the size and scale of its glory days by generations of local people. This raises the question: why have our churches, unlike so many secular buildings, not succumbed to the whims of fashion or the ravages of time?

Matthew Byrne seeks to address this question by taking a magnifying glass to a selection of places of worship, examining their history, their legacy and the craft of those who built and decorated them. His general answer seems to be that these buildings have survived because they are a perfect expression of form matching function; of the merging of the spiritual and the practical. They have remained symbols of reassurance in troubled times. One only has to see the overflowing congregations at Christmas and at times of local and national crisis, to know that churches are still places we turn to when we want to be together.

Matthew Byrne is at pains to show us places of worship of all denominations, as well as all periods. The twentieth-century Roman Catholic church of St Mary, at Leyland in Lancashire, shows how church architecture, design and decoration can still produce something startlingly original.

There has been much talk of the future of our churches as religious observation plays a diminishing part in our daily lives. Almost no-one is suggesting they be knocked down and cleared for car parks. They are still loved and admired, and thanks to bodies like the National Churches Trust, they are finding a new role as venues for concerts, recitals, plays and exhibitions; places of coming together as much as places of worship.

This chimes in with their original function as centres of the community. The more open and welcoming our churches and chapels become, the greater will be the chance of survival, not just for these fine buildings but for the communities they were built to serve.

Michael Palin
London, December 2016

Opposite: The monument to Colonel Cheney at Gaddesby church, Leicestershire, shows him at the Battle of Waterloo where four horses were killed beneath him. He survived until 1848.

Over the years, I have seen the excellent work that the National Churches Trust has undertaken to support and maintain historic church buildings across the United Kingdom.

Keeping churches in good condition is essential for their survival. It allows us to explore the beauty, history and significance of these buildings which provide such vital support to local communities, and to preserve them for future generations.

As Patron of the National Churches Trust, I am pleased to send my warm good wishes to all those who continue to work with and support this splendid charity.

ELIZABETH R.

PREFACE

The National Churches Trust

Churches have been part of local and national landscapes for so many centuries that their presence is often taken for granted. However, ensuring that they remain safeguarded for the future is down to the hard work and dedication of local people and the provision of funding and support. The National Churches Trust and its predecessor charity, the Historic Churches Preservation Trust, are proud to have played a part in keeping churches alive since 1953.

Luke March, Chairman, National Churches Trust

The church of St Mary the Virgin in Alton Barnes, Wiltshire, is one of the smallest in England. Situated between Avebury and Stonehenge, the tiny church, the value of which was put at a mere £5 in 1291, is now considered to be a place of priceless history and beauty. In December 2014, the church was awarded a £20,000 National Churches Repair Grant to help fund a major restoration project including repairs to the roof and dealing with damp in the walls and timberwork.
© Manor Studios

THE NATIONAL CHURCHES TRUST is the national, independent charity dedicated to the repair and support of the UK's churches, chapels and meeting houses. The Trust was created in 2007 to take forward the work of the Historic Churches Preservation Trust, founded in 1953. It does not own any buildings but rather supports those responsible for the upkeep of places of worship.

The Trust has helped virtually every church named in Simon Jenkins' *England's Thousand Best Churches*. Geographically, churches in all four corners of the British Isles have been covered by grants; from St Lawrence, Jersey, to St Magnus, Lerwick in the Shetland Islands, from Christ Church, Lowestoft in Suffolk, to St James, Moy in County Tyrone.

The National Churches Trust's key areas of work include:

1. Keeping churches at the heart of communities in the UK's cities, towns and villages. Many are under threat from leaking roofs, crumbling stonework and rotting timbers. We want to make sure that their architecture and history are there for future generations to enjoy.

   The Trust does this by providing grants for the repair, restoration and maintenance of church buildings, and by supporting projects that enable churches to be at the centre of local communities through the provision of modern facilities such as toilets, kitchens and improving access. Since 2007, we have funded over 2,000 projects at churches, chapels and meeting houses throughout the UK with grants totalling over £19 million.

2. Encouraging regular maintenance of church buildings by providing practical advice, support and information.

   Our MaintenanceBooker website makes it easy for churches, chapels and meeting houses to book maintenance services through accredited and experienced contractors. Simple tasks such as keeping gutters clear and ensuring stonework is well looked after help to keep church buildings in good condition and prevent large repair bills.
   www.maintenancebooker.org.uk

3. Promoting church tourism and bringing a new generation of people into contact with church history and architecture. 'ExploreChurches' (**www.explorechurches.org**) makes it easy to discover the UK's magnificent sacred heritage. The website includes over 3,500 churches with details of opening times, travel information and how to make the most of visiting churches. Getting more people to value our shared heritage of church buildings is a great way of ensuring their long-term sustainability.

4. Working to increase awareness among the public and decision makers of the value of places of worship.

With 'The UK's Favourite Churches' initiative, leading public figures, writers and religious leaders promoted awareness of churches as some of the UK's most important and best-loved buildings and of the need for continuing funding to keep them in good repair for future generations.

Once the centre of Welsh society, many churches and chapels are still vital for community life. Our 'Sacred Wales' – 'Cymru Sanctaidd' campaign celebrated the churches and chapels of Wales and contributed to the debate about their future.

As well as being places of worship, church buildings play an important role in helping local people. It is estimated that nearly 90% of churches are used for community purposes. In '50 Things to do in a Church', the Trust celebrated the many and diverse uses of church buildings and demonstrated their continuing importance to society.

The National Churches Trust receives no income from either government or church authorities and relies on our Friends and supporters to continue our work. You can find out more information about how to support the Trust by visiting our website: **www.nationalchurchestrust.org/support**

The church of All Saints in Evesham, Worcestershire, was awarded a £10,000 National Churches Repair Grant in 2015 to help fund urgent repairs to the stonework of the Bell Tower. It can be seen here during (above © Ian Povey) and after (left © Stan Brotherton) restoration.

MAP OF THE CHURCHES AND CHAPELS

NORTHUMBERLAND

TYNE AND WEAR

DURHAM

CUMBRIA

Brampton **25**

Whitby **20**

NORTH YORKSHIRE

LANCASHIRE

Selby **4**

Beverley **6**

EAST RIDING OF YORKSHIRE

WEST YORKSHIRE

Leyland **26**

Middleton **12**

GREATER MANCHESTER

MERSEYSIDE

Liverpool **24**

SOUTH YORKSHIRE

CHESHIRE

DERBYSHIRE

Well **17**

LINCOLNSHIRE

NOTTINGHAM-SHIRE

Cheadle **22**

STAFFORDSHIRE

SHROPSHIRE

Exton **13**

West Walton **5**

LEICESTERSHIRE

NORFOLK

WEST MIDLANDS

Fotheringhay **10**

Great Witley **16**

CAMBRIDGESHIRE

NORTHAMPTON-SHIRE

Blythburgh **8**

Shobdon **18**

WORCESTER-SHIRE

WARWICK-SHIRE

SUFFOLK

HEREFORDSHIRE

Ripple **7**

BEDFORD-SHIRE

Kilpeck **2**

Tewkesbury **3**

BUCKINGHAM-SHIRE

HERTFORDSHIRE

ESSEX

GLOUCESTERSHIRE

OXFORDSHIRE

City of London **14**

GREATER LONDON

Bradford-on-Avon **1**

BERKSHIRE

KENT

SURREY

Mereworth **15**

WILTSHIRE

HAMPSHIRE

WEST SUSSEX

EAST SUSSEX

Fairfield **19**

SOMERSET

DORSET

Cullompton **9**

DEVON

Altarnun **11**

CORNWALL

St Austell **23**

Come-to-Good **21**

Numbers after place names refer to chapter numbers.

INTRODUCTION

IN SOME 10,000 VILLAGES AND hamlets in every corner of England, the Anglican parish church is both the oldest and the largest building. In some villages it is very large indeed – large enough to seat the congregation of a small town, perhaps five times the entire population of the village (see chapter 8).

Unlike modern architects and their clients, medieval communities did not build simply to accommodate people. The construction of a church was in itself an act of worship – these buildings were created with faith. Most village churches are of a relatively modest size, their rooflines high enough to rise above those of the

As well as being symbolic signposts to heaven, for about 700 years spires like this, which are visible for miles around, have acted as signposts to thousands of English villages and towns, and their bells have rung out across the countryside as a call to prayer, to celebrate and to mourn. This one, which was built c.1300, is at Bredon village, Worcestershire.

surrounding cottages and farmhouses but not high enough to overpower their surroundings, a pleasing mixture of homeliness and 'otherness'. Their most monumental features are their towers and steeples. Travellers are often able to see a country church steeple a mile or two before the village itself is visible. In the flatter countryside of the eastern counties of England, where there can be views of several miles in all directions, it is sometimes possible to see up to six steeples from one spot. This is the country that gave rise to the word 'steeplechasing', as eighteenth-century squires, farmers and young bloods used the church steeples as markers when racing across fields from one village to another. It is still a term used in modern horseracing. John Constable, J. M. W. Turner and many lesser painters saw church towers or steeples as a defining feature of the English landscape, as they still are today.

In hundreds of market towns too, churches are still the largest and oldest buildings. In the nineteenth

In the seventeenth and eighteenth centuries the Roman temple became the model for many churches as design moved away from the soaring Gothic to more earthbound creations. Gunton's 1750 church by Robert Adam is hidden in a park in the heart of rural Norfolk. It would take another 100 years for Gothic to stage a comeback.

century, as many smaller towns grew into large industrial conurbations, this ceased to be true, as factories, warehouses, railway stations and office blocks overshadowed the old churches. Victorian architects responded by building new churches that could compete with industry, creating buildings of a quite different character from that of the homely village churches.

In modern city centres the position is different. The increasing need to build higher and higher creates buildings that dwarf all around them. In the City of London, the ancient Square Mile, even the vast dome of St Paul's Cathedral is overshadowed by its recent neighbours, such as the 'Gherkin', the 'Cheesegrater' and the 'Shard'. Their novel silhouettes on the London skyline have been much admired by professional architects and the general public. Whether they will be admired or even endure for 300 years as St Paul's has done remains to be seen. However, in terms of age the City churches are still the winners. In the shadow of the Tower of London, the church of All Hallows, which escaped the Great Fire of London in 1666, has a crypt, still in use for worship, that is part of the original church built by the monks of Barking Abbey, possibly in the eighth century or a little later. Because of later medieval rebuilding and extensive damage done by bombs in the Second World War, only fragments of Saxon masonry are visible above ground. Like so many English churches, it has always kept pace with the times. It possesses a 1682 font cover that is one of the finest pieces of carving by Grinling Gibbons, some fine eighteenth-century sword rests and several good monuments. Following substantial rebuilding after bomb damage in 1940, many equally good modern pieces of work were commissioned – an altarpiece painting, some bronzes and excellent stained glass in the baptistery created by the leading glazier Keith New in 1964. No other building in London has been continuously used for its original purpose for so long. However, it is not unique; there are many similar churches all over England.

Of course, size and age alone do not make a building beautiful or interesting. From earliest times church building has attracted skilled masons and architects willing and proud to be involved. The names of most of the masons of the early medieval period are either completely unknown or they are known simply as 'Peter of Gloucester' or 'Master William of Canterbury'. In the later Middle Ages we have the names of several of the leaders in their field: Henry Yevele, William Ramsey and William Wynford in the fourteenth century and Richard Winchcombe and John Wastell in the fifteenth century. It was on cathedrals, royal chapels and Oxford colleges, however, that these men mainly worked. In the post-medieval period, Inigo Jones introduced Renaissance architecture to churches in the early seventeenth century. In the later part of that century Christopher Wren, who rebuilt St Paul's Cathedral and the City of London churches after the Great Fire, is considered to be the greatest of all English architects. In the eighteenth century the fashionable architects of the time, who created many great town and country houses, gave their skills to church building: Robert Adam, George Dance, James Gibbs, James Wyatt and others. In the early nineteenth century the father of the Gothic Revival, A. W. N. Pugin, was a committed Christian who built many fine churches (see chapter 22). He was followed by leading architects such as George Gilbert Scott, G. E. Street, William Butterfield, G. F. Bodley, J. L. Pearson and many others. In the late twentieth century and early twenty-first century, churches of all denominations have been prepared to commission the best architects for contemporary-style buildings (see chapter 26).

In 1811 the architect Thomas Rickman first gave names to the periods and styles of English architecture in a classification that has been universally used since then: Anglo-Saxon, Norman, Gothic (Early English, Decorated, Perpendicular) and Classical. This is how the churches covered in this volume will be described in the main text. Here it is sufficient to say that sizes, plans, elevations, ornaments and the overall spirit of places of worship from each era are very different. The earliest Saxon churches were simple two-cell structures with an aisleless nave and a comparatively low and narrow chancel. This layout remained popular for smaller churches throughout the later medieval and post-medieval periods. Although architecturally basic these churches can be lifted to outstanding quality by the use of architectural sculpture, i.e. work integrated into the fabric of the building (see chapter 2). At the other end of the spectrum a grand church will have an aisled nave, a chancel also with aisles, transepts and various chapels in the areas around the chancel. These parts, either individually or in combination, can create thrilling spatial effects that are the especial genius of the architect. A west tower or a crossing tower give the buildings vertical monumentality.

As for art, the interiors of churches have been made beautiful by those who have created the furnishings and fittings: the stained glass artists who made the windows; the carpenters who made the roofs, the rood screens, the carved bench ends and the choir stalls; and the sculptors who made the monuments that recorded the lives and deaths of the great and good – and not so good – over innumerable generations. Modern artists continue to add their skills and imagination to church exteriors and interiors today – glaziers, sculptors, workers in wood and metal and textile designers. This variety of architecture and art in English churches, created over such a long time span, is rare if not unparalleled anywhere else in the world.

The subtitle of this book refers to churches in terms of architecture, art and people and it is the last of these that in the end is the most important. Churches were built by people for the worship of God, and evidence of the divine and human are seen side by side everywhere. People have worshipped in these buildings not only on Sundays; before the Reformation in the sixteenth century the parish priest would celebrate mass daily, attended by the devout who were able to do so, and that practice continues in many places today.

Apart from regular worship churches have seen gatherings of joy when families have met for christenings, weddings, anniversaries and the like and whole communities meet for celebrations such as harvest festivals. They have seen days of deep sorrow as people gathered for funerals. They have seen gatherings marking great national events such as the death and coronation of monarchs. In times of war people have met to sustain national hope and endeavour and celebrate deliverance. All these things have left their visible record in our churches as have deeper and wider changes in religious thinking and attitudes in society.

The most obvious evidence of past generations – at least of the upper and middle classes – is, of course, the monuments. As works of art they can range from the mediocre to the outstanding, when clients have commissioned leading sculptors of the day. However, more than this they reflect the quite different attitudes to life after death and indeed life before death. Bishops, kings, nobility and knights from the Middle Ages lie with their hands piously joined and that is the significance of this form of monument – it implies the deceased, shown in prayer, is asking for God's mercy and forgiveness for themselves and by implication that they are asking for the prayers of the beholders for the deceased's salvation.

In the immediate post-medieval period the monuments grew to enormous size and splendour, with

The changing spirit of post-Reformation monuments.

Top left: A seventeenth-century domestic group at Romsey Abbey, Hampshire. John St Barbe and his wife died on the same day in 1658. Their children are depicted below.

Top Right: Eighteenth-century hauteur at Gayhurst, Buckinghamshire. Sir Nathan Wright and son, erected 1728.

Bottom left: Nineteenth-century pathos at Ledbury, Herefordshire. This monument for the infant John Hamilton, who died in 1851, was shown at the Great Exhibition at Crystal Palace in the same year.

Bottom right: Effigies have disappeared from modern monuments, but this tablet has its own simple dignity telling as it does the story of the last of a family at Ashburnham, Sussex.

architectural surrounds reaching into the very rafters. The use of imported, coloured marble created flashes of brilliance in a dark interior – worldly certainty, but still with a clear feeling of Christian piety, as the deceased lie or now often kneel beneath their canopies. In this and the later Stuart period, busts of the deceased became popular – that of William Shakespeare in the church at Stratford-on-Avon is widely known. Learned men favoured this type of monument, which often featured symbols of their profession around their likeness. In the eighteenth century the style changed dramatically. Full-sized figures in white marble stand erect, dukes, earls and marquises gesticulating to the viewers and beyond them to the lands outside the building, much of which they would have owned and ruled. Spouses and children might be in attendance or allegorical female figures may represent the virtues, real or imagined, of the deceased. With unlimited finance available the finest sculptors in England, such as Louis-Francois Roubiliac or John Michael Rysbrack, were employed. There is a palpable sense of the pride and arrogance of the eighteenth-century nobility in these monuments, where in a more secular age no trace of medieval piety remains. The visitor should not fail to read some of the interminable epigraphs inscribed beneath these figures in which they were attributed with almost every virtue known to man.

In the Victorian period the mood returned to piety combined with pathos. White marble remained the preferred medium, showing young women on deathbeds with grieving husbands alongside or angels hovering above to receive them into eternity. The greatest pathos is in those monuments showing infants in death – a tragedy with which the Victorians were all too familiar. The nobility were invariably buried and commemorated in their own country parish churches, where the stately ancestral home would be only a short distance away. It is common for one family to have so many monuments in their parish church that they fill the chancel (the most prestigious place), the transepts, parts of the nave and special side-chapels, which were built specially to hold them (see chapter 13). It is a remarkable and somewhat ghostly experience to stand alone in a country church in complete silence watched by the eyes of generations of a family, to walk among them and touch them.

The late twentieth century is represented only rarely; the deceased lie outside in the churchyard, not inside. There is neither the inclination nor the money to create monuments of the type described, but small wall tablets engraved with the family coat of arms and a restrained inscription in finely engraved lettering have a simplicity and dignity that in their own way hold their own with the monuments of the past.

The more cheerful world of the living is well represented in wood, stone and glass in churches, and here we are more likely to be given glimpses into the lives of ordinary people rather than the aristocracy. Misericords (the undersides of tip-up choir seats) were widely used to portray medieval life in numerous forms. At Ripple, Worcestershire (see chapter 7), there is a remarkable set of misericords which record the labours of the months. These show simple country folk carrying out the work on a farm between January and December, e.g. collecting firewood in January, sowing in March, reaping in August, spinning and cooking by a fireside in December. These labours appear quite widely. Other misericord subjects involve animals of the countryside, sometimes humorously portrayed, sometimes macabrely; at Malvern, Worcestershire, three rats hang a cat. Foxes and their activities are a popular subject. At Boston, Lincolnshire, school life features in the form of a master caning a schoolboy as his companions look on. Bench ends also provided ample space for the woodcarvers to show their skills in an equally wide variety of subjects, sacred and secular. At Altarnun, Cornwall, there is a jester and a viol player (see chapter 11). Musicians are indeed a common theme, portrayed in stone, wood and stained glass. At Beverley Minster, East Yorkshire (see chapter 6), in the north aisle there is a remarkable sequence of early fourteenth-century stone wall carvings showing ten musicians playing wood, wind and percussion instruments.

Throughout the medieval period, from early Norman times up until the Reformation, little stone heads of every class of person appeared on walls and the capitals of piers; kings, bishops and lay people, some serene and smiling, some serious, some scowling in anger, some grimacing in pain (the sculptor may have had a toothache on that day). The people who financed the extensive stained glass windows sometimes wanted to record their generosity for posterity and stipulated that portraits of themselves should be added at the bases of the windows. These 'donor panels' provide charming cameos of individuals or whole families. The very wealthy sometimes recorded their benefactions in stone. When the great church at Long Melford, Suffolk, was enlarged in the fifteenth century, those who financed the work recorded both their names, the nature of the work and requests for prayers in a

Some old churches preserve memorabilia of former customs.

Top: An eighteenth-century graveside shelter for clergymen at Wingfield, Suffolk.

Bottom: A nineteenth-century glass-sided hearse at Evesham, Worcestershire.

flint frieze above the windows all around the building, giving a nice example of pride and piety combined.

The turmoil of the Reformation has left its mark in almost every church in the country, medieval and post-medieval. The period spans the time of Henry VIII in the sixteenth century to that of the Cromwellian Commonwealth in the seventeenth. It is evident in what is absent and what is present. At the entrances to the church, via a porch at the south end or a door at the west end, there will be several ornate niches that are now empty because the statues that they once held were regarded as 'idolatrous' by the reformers. There will be many more examples of the same thing inside. The large areas of clear glass in a medieval church replaced stained glass that once showed images of saints as well as biblical scenes and legendary miracles. Despite this, a considerable amount that escaped replacement give us an idea of the beauty of much of what was destroyed.

Before the Reformation the chancel, the domain of the clergy, was separated from the nave, the place of the laity, by beautifully carved and ornate rood screens which were in three parts. The screen itself was made up of solid panels in its lower half and open tracery work in its upper part. This supported a rood 'loft' or platform with a parapet, in the middle of which was the rood itself, a large crucifix with the Virgin Mary and St John, the beloved disciple, on either side of Christ. In many cases the entire structure was removed during the reign of Edward VI (r. 1547–53). Frequently, however, the screen section was retained, and occasionally the loft, but all the rood figures were destroyed without exception. The stairways cut in the pillars on either side of the entrance to the chancel leading to the rood loft can still be seen in many places. The lower solid panels of the rood screen were invariably painted with figures of the more popular saints. These were either scraped away completely or only the faces were defaced, leaving the bodies, which are still visible today and can be identified by their traditional symbols painted with them. It is as if the iconoclasts considered the person eliminated if the face were removed. Much work nowadays goes into conserving all these forms of art.

Churches built before the middle of the nineteenth century are also witnesses to the theological changes that occurred during the Reformation. The theology of the reformed church stressed the preaching of the Word (the Bible) over the celebration of the Sacrament (the Eucharist). This showed in the reduction in the status of the chancels, which sometimes became semi-redundant, as the Eucharist might be celebrated only a dozen times a year. At the same time the status of the pulpit grew. Enormous 'three-decker' pulpits were erected in front of the chancel. The lower 'deck' was a seat for the parish clerk, the second was used by the minister (not then referred to as a priest) to read the lesson, while the upper was used for preaching. From this elevated height, some six feet or more above the ground, scholarly eighteenth-century 'divines' would deliver sermons that would be considered to be of prodigious length by modern standards. In London, Oxford, Cambridge and elsewhere these would have been appreciated. Dr Samuel Johnson and his friends were keen 'sermon-tasters' in London, listening to two or three in different churches on Sundays. In rural areas the preaching was probably above the heads of members of the farming communities.

Social attitudes in the eighteenth century are still strikingly visible in some churches, where the seating arrangements show the rigid class distinctions in the community, more perhaps in the country areas than the towns. In a country church close to a stately home, the seating for a duke, earl or marquis and his family might occupy a whole gallery at the west (entrance) end or a transept if that existed. These were equipped with comfortable upholstered seats of the type the family used at home and were sometimes fitted with fireplaces. In the body of the church the nave was filled with separate box pews, each with its own door carrying a brass plate with the name of the family that would occupy it for a yearly rent. The heights of the box pews might be graded with the highest at the front being for the local squire and the rector's family. The lower ones behind were for the prominent farmers and wealthy tradespeople, and those that were lower again would have been for the lower middle classes. At the very back were plain benches for cottage people and farm labourers; these were rent free. For churches newly built in the eighteenth century these things were inserted from the beginning.

Great changes came about in the second half of the nineteenth century. Victorian churchmen rightly disapproved of blatant distinctions in places of worship, and in most churches box pews were swept away and replaced with the standard type of pine benches we know today. Deeper theological changes slowly altered the interiors of the churches yet further. The Oxford Movement, which started in the 1830s, was centred on a group of churchmen who wanted the 'Protestant' element of the Church of England to be replaced by one more connected to its 'Catholic' roots in the Middle Ages. Where these Anglo-Catholic clergy were the incumbents there would be a more frequent celebration of the Eucharist, at least once a week on Sundays, with a greater degree of ceremony in the service in the form of vestments, processions and music. Chancels were re-ordered, with substantial stone altars replacing simple wooden tables, and choir stalls and organs were installed here. The high, three-decker pulpits were replaced with the simpler structures we have today. Plain glass was extensively replaced with stained glass. It was not all of a high quality and the dark colours employed could create a gloomy interior, but the intention was to provide a more religious, devout atmosphere. In the thousands of new churches built in the Victorian era these features could be introduced from the start. In the older, pre-Reformation churches the changes were gradual and slow and met with various degrees of resistance. However, all but a few interiors were re-ordered in this way. The few that were not are mostly in remote country parishes where there was a greater conservatism or a lack of the necessary finance or both. These 'unrestored' churches, as they are known, are a particular joy to visit, and are sought out by regular church explorers. Here the ecclesiastical and social worlds of the seventeenth and eighteenth centuries live on, and they are filled with an atmosphere with which Jane Austen and her clerical characters would be familiar. Of course there are disadvantages as regards modern worship. High box pews do not provide the

As well as building many outstanding churches the modern age is continually commissioning new works of art from leading artists. A popular choice is stained glass such as *Christ Crucified* (below), installed in 2000 at Bunbury, Cheshire.

sense of community and sharing in a church that is thought natural today, and they and the uneven stone-flagged floors must be a nightmare for those who have to do the cleaning.

In the later nineteenth century it was often necessary to carry out major building work on the older medieval churches for practical rather than ideological reasons. These buildings were often deplorably neglected throughout the eighteenth century, partly because in an age when Classical architecture was fashionable, Gothic was despised, and partly due to an underlying coolness towards religion. A single service of matins on a Sunday morning might be the only weekly worship. By the 1850s many old churches were crumbling. From the early twentieth century repair work on an ancient building would be approached from the viewpoint of scholarly and sensitive 'conservation' rather than 'restoration', the aim being to respect the architectural and historical integrity of the building. At the time 'restoration' would often involve the demolition and rebuilding of an entire chancel, aisle or tower or in some cases of virtually an entire church. What was rebuilt often bore little resemblance to what had been there originally.

The Victorians had decided views on what constituted 'good' and 'bad' architectural styles. They regarded the first (Early English) period of Gothic architecture as 'immature', and the third and last (Perpendicular) period was regarded as 'debased'. Only the Middle Pointed, or Decorated Gothic, was regarded as reaching perfection, and restored features or sections of a church were rebuilt as a reproduction of that period. As a result, many nominally medieval churches bear little resemblance to the originals, externally or internally. It is the constant work of the architectural historian to work out what is old and what is not. In fairness to the Victorians, many churches would not exist today without their well-meaning, if over-zealous, interventions.

John Wesley (1703–91) was an ordained minister in the Church of England when he underwent a personal spiritual experience that called him to a more personal relationship with Jesus Christ. Concerned about what he saw as spiritual apathy and coolness within the Church of England, he felt called also to bring his personal experience to others, which he did in a lifetime of travelling and preaching throughout the country. Initially he continued to worship and preach in parish churches, but as a rift with the Anglican establishment widened he preached first in the open air and then in purpose-built chapels. This movement of 'Methodism' gained widespread support in places as diverse as Cornish villages and the growing industrial towns of northern England. The smaller buildings in Cornwall, where some 700 were built, justified the name of 'chapel', but in the towns buildings to seat up to 1,000 people were required. They were likewise known as 'chapels' to satisfy laws requiring a distinction from the Anglican parish church. A mid-nineteenth-century Methodist governing body decreed that the architecture should be based on 'beauty and perfection and executed without unnecessary adornment'. Big town chapels, which are usually faced with stone, have a sober solemnity that adequately asserts their presence alongside the parish churches. The inspirational preaching of John Wesley influenced their interiors, where the ground-level pews and galleries on three sides all focussed on a tall pulpit raised on a dais. Modern Methodist buildings, now churches rather than chapels, are generally indistinguishable from contemporary Anglican and Roman Catholic buildings. They and other chapels in the United Reformed, Baptist and other traditions are also supported by the National Churches Trust.

At the sixteenth-century Reformation Roman Catholics were forbidden to take part in public worship, such as the celebration of mass. Following the Acts of Catholic Emancipation between 1790 and 1830 the prohibition was lifted, and Roman Catholic churches appeared in increasing numbers throughout the nineteenth century. The patrons who financed them were often wealthy recusant aristocrats building for their fellow English Catholics and the large number of Irish immigrants. Such men could afford to give outstanding architects such as A. W. N. Pugin full rein in the creation of magnificently ornate buildings (see chapter 22). Although early churches were often based on classical Italianate models befitting the link with Rome, Pugin was the passionate advocate of a return to the medieval Gothic style. He believed that this, and not the pagan temples of Ancient Rome and Greece, was the only proper form for Christian churches. His views laid the foundation for the Gothic Revival movement of the later nineteenth century which was widely adopted in all Christian denominations. Roman Catholic churches are also supported by the National Churches Trust.

Thousands of English churches are situated in places where the pleasure of visiting them involves the additional enjoyment of journeys to some of the most beautiful, exciting – and surprising – places in England. The spectrum is immense. Some are in remote, secret places where they may stand completely alone. To reach

Brougham church (Ninekirks) in Cumbria visitors must park their cars beside the main Appleby to Penrith road in open rolling countryside and take a footpath that runs alongside the River Eamont, whose red sandstone banks glow brightly in the sunlight. The land soon rises a little to give a view of a medium-sized, low, ground-hugging church surrounded by its churchyard in the middle of a large field where there is no other building in sight. Visitors to Badley church in Suffolk again leave a main road and follow a rutted cart track for a mile before seeing a tower and the upper part of a church hidden with its churchyard in a circle of trees in the centre of a common. In an island with thousands of miles of coastline there have always been isolated communities living off the sea. In south Cornwall the lonely church at Gunwalloe is surrounded only by sand dunes a few yards above the high tide mark. In the north of that county the equally lonely church at Morwenstow is on the edge of a cliff overlooking the Atlantic Ocean. A number of churches stand alone or almost alone on the tops of steep hills. At the village of Richards Castle in Shropshire the houses are at the bottom of a hill, while the Norman castle that gives the village its name is sited at the top for defensive reasons. The castle chapel, which has been enlarged to become the parish church, lies alongside with just three cottages as neighbours. The views from here stretch over three counties. The village of Breedon-on-the-Hill in Leicestershire is really 'Breedon-under-the-Hill' because the only building on the hill is the large parish church with its wonderful collection of Saxon sculpture. The builders of these and similar churches never foresaw such isolation. Medieval people had no regard for picturesque surroundings when siting a church for the practical purpose of worship. Isolation has arisen from the disappearance of the original villages due to plague, flooding or a change in the agricultural policies of wealthy landowners. Particularly fascinating, however, are those churches that *were* built to stand and be seen alone in the parks of great country houses (see chapter 17).

In rural England the centre of a village is the natural and usual home of a parish church. The village may be readily accessible, on or near a main road, or it may be reached only by travelling along miles of narrow winding lanes. The church and its churchyard, a beautiful and interesting place in its own right, may be at the centre of the village, surrounded on all sides by cottages, farmhouses or grander houses. Often it is at the edge of the village where its churchyard adjoins the houses on one side and open fields on the others in a wonderful meeting of habitation, worship and agriculture.

Every market town will have a church, usually sited at the historic centre. That church will be surrounded by houses and inns nearly as old as itself and many later Georgian streets lined with houses that have that simple unfussy elegance that only the eighteenth century could create.

The suburbs of the larger towns and the cities where many fine Victorian churches were built (see chapter 24) may be less exciting places to visit unless one shares the enthusiasm of the late Sir John Betjeman for suburbia. City centre churches, on the other hand, often have vibrant and exciting surroundings. The cathedral-like fourteenth-century church of St Mary Redcliffe in Bristol presides over what might be described as England's answer to Venice, where the winding River Avon and its side-cuts are lined with quays, old docks, striking modern blocks of flats and shops, between which people are ferried by small boats throughout the day. In the centre of Manchester the elegant eighteenth-century church of St Anne forms one complete side of the eponymous square which is the most fashionable and busy shopping area of the city. In the City of London, the late seventeenth-century churches of Sir Christopher Wren have perhaps the most extraordinary and thrilling urban surroundings in England, hemmed in by solid nineteenth-century commercial buildings, which are often in physical contact with them. Their close neighbours are the ultra-high futuristic buildings of the late twentieth and early twenty-first centuries. Although they are far less tall, the exquisitely elegant and playful Baroque steeples of a genius architect enliven the City skyline in quite a different way and show that God and Mammon can co-exist, physically at least, in this centre of world money. Of all the City churches St Stephen Walbrook (see chapter 14) has perhaps the busiest site of all, where the junction of six major thoroughfares is ringed by three historic buildings: the huge masses of the Bank of England, the Royal Exchange and the Mansion House, the official home of the Lord Mayor. In the middle of this, cars, taxis and buses circulate bumper to bumper from dawn to dusk. Only on Saturdays and Sundays does an eerie calm descend.

From lonely, secretive Brougham, seen only by those prepared to hike over north country fells, to the bustling centre of England's financial heart a truly remarkable series of contrasts can be seen. Those who have explored English churches have explored England.

Churches have been described in terms of their antiquity, their architecture, their works of art and the people who have used them in the past, which brings us to the all important people of our own time, for despite occasional remarks to the contrary churches are places of the living present. Over two million people attend services in Christian churches and chapels on a regular weekly basis and many more attend the greater festivals. These people are therefore irritated that churches are regarded by some solely as repositories of fine art and social history, and a book of this type may do nothing to dispel that idea. Architecture and artworks, however, provide little incentive for those making their way to an early morning Communion Service on a Sunday in the middle of winter and taking their places in a building that may have an under-powered heating system. Christians certainly take pride in their churches, both ancient and modern, and in the fact that worship in some of them has taken place continuously for centuries. They know, however, that these things would be for nothing if they did not continue to be places of Christian spirituality in the way of prayer, learning, meditation and sacraments as well as good fellowship.

In addition to those who worship in them churches welcome about ten million visitors from home and abroad each year, some on an occasional basis and some for whom churches are a lifelong interest. The essential vocation of Christian clergy is to act as the spiritual leaders and guides of their people but they also have the enormous – and at times worrying – task, together with their church wardens and other helpers, of caring for the upkeep of churches and chapels and their contents for the whole community. Some Anglican clergy in country areas are charged with looking after six or more ancient churches where things such as roofs, windows, towers and many other features are constant problems requiring time and expense. Modern buildings too are not without their problems. It is for these things that clergy are able to turn to the National Churches Trust for financial help and advice, and its work is vital for the present and future upkeep of innumerable ancient buildings. It deserves the support of as many people as possible (see page 191).

English churches represent 1,300 years of Christian faith during which time artists have expressed the same beliefs in the idiom of their time. There are no better examples than the Saxon Madonna and Child at Inglesham, Wiltshire (left), and that by Henry Moore, 1944 (right), at Northampton. Although separated by 1,000 years both have captured the same sense of tender love between Mary and the Christ Child. In the Saxon work the Hand of God points to His Son.

THE ANGLO-SAXON CENTURIES, 700–1066

Churches Built During the Birth of the English Nation

THERE ARE ABOUT 500 CHURCHES in England that predate the Norman Conquest, either wholly or in part. There is something in the English psyche that is drawn to these churches, which link the current generations to the beginnings of a nation before the arrival of the Normans. In places that have a Saxon church the local people often seem proud to proclaim it. In many villages a little wooden finger signpost will point down a lane 'to the Saxon church', or on a main road a major sign will indicate a turning to a village that advertises its Saxon church.

They were not the first Christian churches in England. In the last 100 years of the Roman occupation of Britain, before the troops withdrew in 410, there was a significant Christian presence here after the Emperor Constantine first legalised Christianity by the Edict of Milan in 313 and later made it the official religion of the empire. The faith hardly survived the departure of the Romans except on the far western fringes, and only scant archaeological traces remain to testify to the presence of churches in towns and forts and private chapels in country villas.

Christianity returned to Britain 200 years later, starting in two far-distant, opposite corners of the island. In 597 St Augustine and his Benedictine monks landed in Kent on a mission ordered by Pope Gregory the Great. At about the same time monks from the abbey at Iona off the west coast of Scotland, which had been founded by the Irish St Columba in 562, started sending their brethren into the north-west of England. From these two starting points Christianity spread slowly and fitfully through a land that was not yet a united nation. The regional kings in Kent and

Northumbria were converted first, followed by those in Mercia, which covered modern central England, and Wessex, covering the south-west. This meant there were two ethnically and culturally different influences at work – Irish Celtic and that of mainland Europe based on Rome.

The Saxon kings, bishops and monks were in regular contact with Europe, travelling through Germany and France on their way to Rome or further afield to the Holy Land. The churches that they would have seen and worshipped in were being built in an early form of what later became known as Romanesque architecture derived from the architecture of Imperial Rome in so far as that was known and understood. Inside them aisled structures were based on round-headed arches supported by circular columns leading up to roofs with Roman systems of stone vaulting. Doors and windows were framed by the same type of round arches. In England the available knowledge and technical skills brought back by travellers created churches that were only echoes of the continental models, themselves a more distant echo of classical Rome.

Most Saxon churches are small 'two-cell' structures of nave and chancel, without aisles, because the latter would have involved the building of wide arches whose stability would have required greater skills than builders accustomed to working in wood could have possessed. For the same reason arches separating the chancel from the nave, doors and windows were all made extremely narrow to reduce the danger of collapse. A curious feature of small Saxon churches is their great height compared with their width. Towers are rare but where they do occur they can be impressive, with stone pilasters attached to the surface to imitate the framework of timber buildings. The round towers of East Anglia are an interesting regional variation. Whatever their limitations in architecture there were schools of highly skilled stone sculptors whose work adorns many churches (see chapter 1) and free-standing crosses. The abundance of abstract interlace and knot work shows the Celtic influence in the Saxon world, but excellent, and often moving, figure sculpture is not uncommon. These features, singly or together, may help to identify a pre-conquest church.

Saxon artists were also highly skilled in metalwork, including gold and silver work. Adorned with precious stones from as far afield as Asia Minor and India, this metalwork was used to create religious objects for churches, personal jewellery and military weapons, as seen in the 'hoards' regularly excavated, most recently the Staffordshire Hoard in 2009. The monks of Saxon monasteries produced masterpieces of illuminated books such as the Lindisfarne Gospels for use in churches. While such items as these can only now be seen in museums and libraries, they are a reminder that the Saxon churchmen were people of advanced learning and culture as well as of piety. From the time of Augustine to the later Saxon kings, notably Alfred and his successors, they were not only present at the birth of England, but they also helped to bring about that birth by working to form a system of unified government based on efficient administration, education, law and justice.

Saxon sculpture is often more accomplished than the architecture of the period. The cross shaft in the remote village of Bewcastle, Cumbria, shows (top to bottom) the figures of St John the Evangelist, Christ and St John the Baptist. Carved c.700–750, 'there is nothing as perfect of a comparable date in Europe'.

1
ST LAWRENCE, BRADFORD-ON-AVON, WILTSHIRE

A Moving Reminder of Distant Saxon Forebears

BRADFORD-ON-AVON IS AN ATTRACTIVE SMALL town about five miles south-east of Bath. The River Avon runs through its centre and is crossed by a bridge dating back to the thirteenth century, with a former medieval chapel in its middle. In the Middle Ages the town thrived on the same woollen industry that brought prosperity to the adjacent Cotswolds and continued to do so into later centuries. The result is a wealth of elegant seventeenth- and eighteenth-century houses and some impressive mansions. The extensive

The north view shows the full ground plan of the original church: chancel, nave and porticus.

use of the local cream-coloured limestone gives the town centre a visual harmony. On the north side of the river the land rises steeply, so that when viewed from below the houses at each level seem to stand on the roofs of those below.

In Church Street, close to the river, there is not one church but two. The large parish church of Holy Trinity has traces of Norman work, but the church is now mainly of the fourteenth and fifteenth centuries. Only a few yards away is the small Saxon church of St Lawrence whose survival is little short of a miracle. When the Normans occupied an existing Saxon settlement the church was either demolished and rebuilt or simply extended, usually leaving some traces of its previous history. In Bradford-on-Avon, St Lawrence's was left intact and a much larger Norman church was built nearby. The former Saxon church would then have become redundant and at some unknown time it was converted into a cottage with a schoolroom attached. Its origin was discovered in 1856 by the then vicar of Bradford-on-Avon. Fortunately, it was not beyond return to its original use and this was done under scholarly supervision in 1870–90.

As with almost all Saxon churches it is hard to date the building accurately. The historian-monk

William of Malmsbury (c.1090–1143) recorded that St Aldhelm (640–709), bishop of Shaftesbury and leading intellectual of his time, founded a monastery at Bradford-on-Avon and a monastery is mentioned in a deed of 705. However, it cannot be proved that these documents refer to the present church. If so it would be an example of very early Saxon Christianity in England. Some architectural evidence in the building itself suggests a rather later date (see page 29).

The building is a perfect example of a small Saxon church containing all the main features of the period described previously. The nave is conspicuously tall compared with its width. The separate chancel is lower and narrower. On each side of the nave there was originally a porticus or side-chamber. They appear now as porches but had more significance than that. Their purpose seems to have varied: as side-chapels, places for burial or relics, or as meeting rooms. The one on the south side disappeared during the time the church was used as a cottage but that on the north side survives in its entirety, if somewhat time-damaged.

Opposite: The little church was built between 100 and 300 years before the Norman Conquest. This south side view shows the tall, narrow proportions typical of many Saxon churches. A former porticus, or side-chamber, between the modern buttresses has disappeared.

27

It has a doorway on the outer front, typically narrow in the Saxon way. The pilasters with crude block capitals that surround it are a faint echo of the buildings of Imperial Rome.

Inside, the high, narrow proportions are even more keenly felt. The arch leading into the chancel is little more than a doorway in its narrowness. The Saxon masons could not risk a wider arch head for fear of collapse. Above it are the reasonably well preserved remains of part of a rood. Two angels sculpted in low relief swing censers on either side of a gap where the crucifix would have been. This feature was to become a prominent and highly developed wooden feature in front of medieval chancels where images of the Virgin

In the north porticus, the narrow round-arched doorway with side pilasters is a dimly perceived version of ancient Roman architecture.

Above, left: The nave looking east emphasises the height and narrowness of the church. The doorway-sized arch leads into a cell-like chancel.

Below, left: Above the chancel arch two angels swing censers on either side of a now missing crucifix.

Above, right: The view from the north porticus into the nave catches the claustrophobic atmosphere of the church.

Mary and St John stood on either side of the crucified Christ mounted on an ornate rood screen. In length and width the chancel beyond is little more than a small domestic room. The interior has been sparingly fitted with a few furnishings appropriate to the period, including an altar and hanging oil lamps.

It can be seen from the photograph of the south side (see page 26) that in the area between the two string courses there is a line of 'blank arcading' or recesses cut out of the stonework. This is indicative of late rather than early Saxon architecture, perhaps that of the tenth century. Some scholars therefore believe that the church is of that time rather than that of Bishop Aldhelm. Others believe that a church of c.700 may have been embellished at a later date.

Details of dates and architecture apart, the claustrophobia induced by thick walls enclosing the tiny nave, chancel and porticus gives the impression of a building sheltering its beleaguered people from a hostile world of forest, marsh and hills outside.

ENGLAND UNDER NORMAN RULE, 1066–1200

Churches Exuding the Power of the Conquerors Rise up Throughout England

THE NORMANS CONQUERED AND SUBDUED the Anglo-Saxon people of England using physical force, and their innumerable castles reflect their power. Their churches too, small as well as large, have the same overpowering presence, as though their aim was to impress and even intimidate in the spiritual as well as the temporal sphere. These buildings reflect the structure of the Norman state, both in Normandy and England, which had two interlocked arms: the secular based on the king and nobles, and the ecclesiastical based on the senior clergy, archbishops, bishops and abbots. It is no accident that

Warfare and whimsy are just two in the remarkable range of subjects in Norman figure sculpture.

Left: Two knights, one with a sword, the other with a lance, in a vicious battle on the *c.*1150 font at Eardisley, Herefordshire. The symbolism of the subject is obscure.

Opposite: Watched by a man, a donkey and a monkey carry a baby hare in a hod at Barfeston, Kent, *c.*1180.

in cities, towns and villages, large or small churches often lie immediately adjacent to large or small castles. The extent of Norman building was prodigious. Within a generation of the Conquest it stretched from the southern coast to the Scottish border and from the Welsh border to the east coast.

The Normans were a northern Viking people who arrived in Normandy in 950 and gave that area of France their name. They were pagans but quickly assimilated Catholic Christianity under the popes. In the tenth and eleventh centuries western Europe had developed a technically and aesthetically sophisticated form of architecture based on that of Imperial Rome that was consequently known as 'Romanesque'. The leaders of this architectural development were the architects, masons and sculptors of the great cathedrals and abbeys, buildings of unprecedented size and grandeur. Complex ground plans with aisled naves, transepts, elaborate chancels and many chapels rose up in three- or four-storey elevations. The builders employed the constructional techniques of ancient Rome where broad, round-headed arches were supported on massive piers and massively thick walls supported stone-vaulted roofs. Figure sculpture featured prominently externally on facades, but decoration was used sparingly inside where the overwhelming scale and the enclosing presence of plain thick walls are the elements that impress.

The Normans made the style their own in Normandy and brought it to England with even greater effect in cathedrals, abbeys and large and small parish churches. Hence, Romanesque architecture in England is widely known as Norman architecture. Their churches overawe today as much as they must have done 900 years ago. Their massiveness is reflected in walls that are up to 12 feet thick in major buildings and commonly six feet or more in smaller churches. Aisled buildings are supported by elephantine piers up to 15 feet in diameter. The atmosphere in a Norman church is one of earthy austerity as in the great hall of an adjacent castle, although today that may be softened by brightly coloured Victorian floor tiles and other modern furnishings.

Decoration is provided on doorways, windows, the arches in aisles and the capitals of piers in an abundance of both abstract geometrical decoration and figure sculpture. The former employs the ubiquitous zig-zag or chevron and a variety of other forms. Undoubtedly, these have the barbarism of a people not long distanced from the far north of Europe, but it impresses with the vitality it exudes. The figure sculpture has an equally wide variety of forms: naturalistic animals, grotesque creatures from Norse mythology together with sacred (and sometimes far from sacred) human representations. Complex mixtures of both were often put together with considerable compositional skill. This was done in places where they would be most conspicuous – the main entrances to a church or the chancel arch, which the congregation would be facing during a service.

The Normans invested heavily in monasticism in England as they did in Normandy where dukes and barons vied with each other to found great monasteries. The churches of several of these survived the dissolution and looting of the monasteries by Henry VIII in the 1530s when they became parish churches, which today are among the finest we have. The three chapters that follow describe one small and two very large Norman churches that speak eloquently of the character of the remarkable people who built them.

2
ST MARY AND ST DAVID, KILPECK, HEREFORDSHIRE

'One of the Most Perfect Norman Village Churches in England'

THE ENGLISH–WELSH BORDERLAND, THE Marches, was an area of particular concern and importance to William the Conqueror and his successors as they defended their newly conquered English kingdom from the yet unconquered Welsh. The name 'Marches' comes from the Anglo-Saxon word *mearc*, meaning boundary, in the special sense of one that is disputed. Before the Normans the Saxons too had had their conflicts with the Welsh, as illustrated by the dyke built by King Offa of Mercia along most of the

The chancel has an apse (a semicircular eastern extension) based on the earliest Christian churches of fourth-century Rome.

Opposite: Although the church is remote, small and structurally simple, the sculptural work of 1120–50 on every part of the exterior and interior is outstanding by both national and European standards.

length of the border between England and Wales. In the eleventh and twelfth centuries the Normans built a large number of castles along approximately the same line, from Chester in the north to Cardiff in the south. Some of them, such as Chester, Shrewsbury, Ludlow and Chepstow, were massive fortresses. Others were of more moderate size, and scores of others were built small and remained small. The latter never extended beyond minor motte-and-bailey structures, watching posts as it were for the bigger places. William gave lands here to his powerful and trustworthy earls and barons, known as the Marcher Lords, who took charge of this line of defence.

Despite their ruthless militarism the Normans were a committed Christian people and the castles built by the Marcher Lords had churches or chapels within or adjacent to them. The smaller, remoter places had correspondingly small two-compartment churches of nave and chancel only. Architecturally many of these are insignificant. Their fame in England and throughout Europe lies in the related field of architectural sculpture. From 1120 to 1160 the Norman overlords employed a small group of sculptors whose technical skill was matched by their artistic imagination and knowledge of a wide range of biblical, classical and European sources as well as Saxon and Celtic ones closer to home. The Marcher Lords were men of little or no learning but they employed as estate stewards, advisors and chaplains men of advanced education who had lived in Normandy and travelled across France, Spain and Italy, some of them going as far as Jerusalem. In England they were moreover in constant contact with senior clergy, bishops and abbots who were learned in ecclesiastical art. The sculptors, given the advice and resources of men like these, produced a wealth of architectural sculpture of such quality and extent that it is known as the Herefordshire School of Romanesque (or Norman) Sculpture. They used the type of abstract geometrical decoration found elsewhere in England but their particular skill was figure sculpture.

The little church at Kilpeck is the finest of their churches. Kilpeck is a mere hamlet about seven miles south-west of the cathedral city of Hereford.

It is hidden in a quiet and secret part of perhaps the quietest and most secret county in England. Despite its relative inaccessibility a steady trickle of amateur and professional photographers has made it one of the most photographed small churches in England. Today the church is surrounded by a small group of cottages to the south and east and open countryside to the north. Immediately to the west, half-buried in shrubs and trees, are the remains of a small castle. After the Conquest, Kilpeck was given by William to the fitz Norman family. They first built a motte-and-bailey castle, with the wooden structure on the motte being replaced by a stone keep in the twelfth century.

No exact dates are available for the building of the church. It was probably constructed around 1135–40 in the time of Hugh fitz Norman, who endowed a small Benedictine priory here as a cell of the great abbey at Gloucester. Between castle and priory, therefore, there would have been ample funds and expertise for the building of a small but spectacular church. Although, as stated, most of these small churches in the Marches are two-compartment buildings of nave and chancel, Kilpeck is unusual in having a semicircular extension, an apse, leading beyond the chancel. This model is based on Early Christian period practice and shows that the patrons were familiar with European churches of that time.

The church is built of the local Old Red Sandstone, which on a sunny day glows as if on fire. The path from the churchyard gate leads directly to the south door, which is one of the most lavishly decorated in England and, as a tour-de-force, is an appropriate introduction to the church. Moreover, the subject matter of the decorations is of rare and exceptional interest. Immediately to the left and right of the door two plain jambs support a decorated lintel. Above this is a tympanum, a flat semicircular stone spanning the width of the door. Such a conspicuous place was often used by the Normans for pieces of significant sculpture. Here it is carved with a Tree of Life with rather sparse foliage and bunches of grapes. It may represent the tree God planted in the Garden of Eden (Genesis, 2:9) or that in the Book of Revelation (22:2) or Christ's reference to himself as the True Vine (John, 15:1). The door jambs are flanked on each side by two shafts, the inner ones wider that the outer. The shafts to the left are especially interesting. The wider one has two knights standing one upon the other enmeshed in foliage trails. The lower knight carries a sword, the one above a cross. This could be a specific reference to Kilpeck, where

a castle and church stand adjacent to one another, but it could also be a symbolic reference to the Church and the Crown as the two sources of authority in the Norman state. The knights have exaggeratedly long, wiry figures and narrowly pointed heads. They wear caps associated with Phrygia in Asia Minor and on their bodies are hauberk coats of mail and loose-fitting trousers held up by rope belts. Alongside them, on the thinner shaft, two long, fat snakes slither downwards, one biting the tail of the other. The knights could represent the powers of good, conquering animals taken as symbols of evil ever since the Garden of Eden (Genesis, 3:1–5).

The tympanum is surrounded by three concentric arches. The inner is decorated with a simple zig-zag,

Kilpeck has the most famous and most photographed church doorway in England. The wealth of sculpture is varied and complex. Much of it has learned scriptural and theological significance. In the semicircular tympanum is the Tree of Life representing Christ.

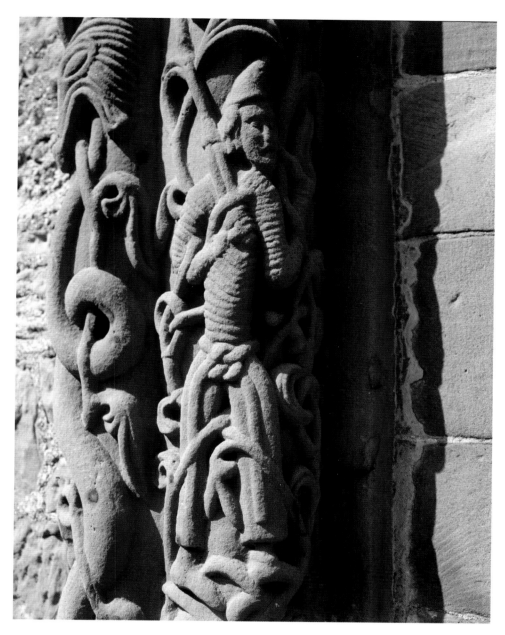

Much scholarly research has attempted to identify the sources from which all these carvings derive. *The Bestiary* has already been referred to; Hugh fitz Norman may have seen the copy at Hereford Cathedral. Strong resemblances between various Kilpeck carvings and major churches elsewhere indicate that the Kilpeck sculptors had worked in these places or visited them: Hereford and Gloucester cathedrals, Reading Abbey (a prestigious building whose patron was Henry I) and Tewkesbury Abbey (see chapter 3). The dragons are from Viking art. The thin folds of the knights' drapery may also be of pre-Conquest Celtic style or taken from regional Roman sculpture. The way in which the knights stand above one another (as do the saints in the chancel arch, see page 37) has been compared with churches in western France and the pilgrimage church of St James at Santiago de Compostella.

The entire building has a projecting line of stone, a corbel table, beneath the roof that helps to support the roof timbers. It is decorated with no fewer than 89 human and animal heads, which are as full of symbolism as the south door. Only a few can be described and shown. Centrally, at the east end of the apse and hence immediately outside the altar, is an *Agnus Dei* (Christ as the Lamb of God) with a

The interlace decoration on a west window shows Celtic and Saxon influences.

One of the supporting side shafts of the doorway shows an armed warrior with helmet and pantaloons. Behind him snakes slither up and down another shaft.

in this case at right angles to the wall, a late Norman motif. The centre arch has at its apex an angel carrying a scroll, showing it is a messenger of God. To its left and right is a semicircle of 'beakheads', grotesque mythical animals pointing down and biting into the moulding below. Much of the animal figure sculpture at Kilpeck and elsewhere is taken from *The Bestiary*, originally an illustrated Greek book depicting real and imaginary animals which churchmen of the early Middle Ages used to create a series of allegorical connections with bible stories and teaching. Thus the phoenix to the left of the angel is a symbol of the Resurrection. The other arch is decorated with a series of medallions containing ferocious dragons' heads and birds such as cocks and eagles, all of which have scriptural significance.

The aisleless three-compartment interior is defined by arches from nave to chancel and chancel to apse.

human-lion head to the left and a human head with a pencil moustache to the right. Also on the apse is the head of an ibex apparently placed upside down by mistake. If so it is incredible that it would not have been corrected immediately. It has been suggested that this has a symbolic meaning taken from *The Bestiary*, which describes the strong horns of an ibex as bearing the full weight of its body as it falls headlong down a rock face, thus saving it. This is an allegory of a good man who when in danger is saved by the two 'horns' of the Bible: the Old and the New Testament. To the left of the ibex is a bald head with a goatee beard and upturned moustache. To its right is a double portrait of a hound and a hare which look as though they might have been taken from a modern comic or cartoon film. Medieval masons did indeed

have a keen sense of humour but again symbolism may be intended. *The Bestiary* describes a dog as the most understanding of all animals, which serves its master by barking warnings just as Christian preachers do, and the hare as representing God-fearing men.

At the west end of the nave is a richly decorated original Norman window (several of the others were replaced during the Gothic periods). It has an inner arch with interlace in the Celtic or Saxon traditions.

The interior is small and coolly uncluttered so that the most prominent and ornate feature, the chancel arch, strikes the visitor with special force. Beyond that there is the arch into the apse, and beyond that again another arch surrounding the far east window, which creates an interesting receding vista. The chancel arch has the standard Norman zig-zag but the figure

sculpture on the jambs is as interesting as that on the south door. On each side are three saints standing on top of each other. Only one, the central figure on the north side, can be identified, as it is clearly St Peter with the key of the Kingdom of Heaven in one hand and a book in the other. It has been suggested that the figure above him may be St David, co-patron of the church; he holds a cross in his right hand and again a book in the other. These figures differ markedly from the knights on the south door. Whereas the latter are tall with thin heads, the chancel arch saints are short and stocky and they have round or ovate heads with huge bulging eyes and drooping moustaches which give them gloomy expressions. The draperies on the knights and saints are also different. For this reason it is generally believed that their sculptors were different.

The arch that leads into the apse is by contrast quite plain but the apse itself is notable in that the semi-dome of the roof has stone rib vaulting, whereas the roofs of the nave and chancel are timber. Rib vaulting appeared in England for the first time in 1093 at Durham Cathedral. The fact that it was used at Kilpeck little more than a generation later shows how close to the architectural forefront its designers were.

Those who become interested in the Herefordshire School of Norman Sculpture can visit other outstanding examples in the villages of Shobdon (see chapter 18), Rowlestone, Eardisley, Castle Frome, Aston Eyre and elsewhere. A tour of the Marches provides a combination of unique architecture and quietly beautiful landscapes.

Left: A pier of the chancel arch shows St Peter with a key below and another saint, perhaps St David of Wales, above.

Below: Two of the 89 corbel carvings that can be seen all around the church.

Right: At the centre the Lamb of God with two faces on either side.

Left: At the centre an inverted head of an ibex with a moustachioed head left and a cartoon-like rabbit and dog right. The inverted head is not an error. Like the other figures it has theological significance (see page 36).

3
THE ABBEY CHURCH OF ST MARY, TEWKESBURY, GLOUCESTERSHIRE

A Norman Monastic Church Splendidly Enriched by Later Generations

THE TOWN OF TEWKESBURY IN north Gloucestershire lies on the bank of the River Avon close to its confluence with the River Severn. The town sprang up, as did many others, around a Norman abbey. The historic centre consists of a number of narrow lanes and alleys leading off a long, winding high street. Its lengthy history has resulted in a remarkable number of diverse domestic buildings. The Middle Ages are represented by several timber-framed houses and inns dating back to the fourteenth century,

their presence made more prominent by the upper storeys overhanging the narrow streets. The seventeenth century is well represented and the eighteenth century even more so in houses ranging from cottages to the mansions of wealthy clothiers and other merchants. Little has been added since 1850, although modern shop fronts at ground level obscure the antiquity of some of the buildings above and behind them.

A small Saxon monastery existed here before the Conquest. Robert Fitzhamon, a Norman nobleman, founded the present Benedictine abbey in 1092. This was very much in the Norman tradition, which contrived to combine an aggressive militarism with Christian piety. The abbey church was completed in 1121 and after that development of the monastery continued under Robert Fitzroy, Earl of Gloucester, an illegitimate son of Henry I. The lands around Tewkesbury later came into the hands of the de Clare and Despenser families, who financed the architectural changes in the church in the later Middle Ages and who are commemorated within by many fine monuments. At the suppression of the monastery by Henry VIII in 1539 the townspeople, who were already using the nave for parish services, bought the entire church from the Crown. The other buildings, except for a gatehouse and the abbot's house, have disappeared almost entirely.

The church consists of a nave with aisles, transepts with a central crossing tower and a chancel. The latter is surrounded by a semicircular passage giving access to a series of radiating chapels. This arrangement, a chevet, was standard for the great Romanesque abbeys in Normandy and elsewhere in France. The overall ground plan is therefore one of considerable complexity. Its size can be judged by the fact that its dimensions are almost identical to those of Westminster Abbey. A good view of the whole building is shown in the photograph taken from the south-east (see page 38). The crossing tower is 'probably the largest and finest Romanesque tower in England'. The upper part is in three stages, the upper and lower of which contain the bell-openings with blank arches on either side. Between them is a band of continuous narrow blank arches. It is a typically busy Norman composition. At the west end of the church the original entrance to the nave is contained within a giant 65-foot recessed arch, 'one of the finest original Norman fronts now existing'. The window within is from the sixteenth century and is a copy of an earlier original.

The interior of the nave is a remarkable synthesis of two very disparate features, each individually impressive but combined in an awkwardly forced marriage. Below is the Norman arcade of cylindrical piers of typically elephantine appearance, six and a half feet in diameter and exuding typically Norman might. These originally supported a wooden roof that was replaced by a fine stone-ribbed roof in 1340. However, the connection with the Norman work below is too abrupt to be aesthetically harmonious. Moreover, the roof is set so low that it appears to crush the arcade while at the same time obscuring much of the Norman fenestration. The resulting lack of daylight is compensated for today by upward floodlighting of the roof.

The east end of the church, the chancel and the Norman chevet were much altered and beautified by the de Clare and Despenser families in the mid-fourteenth century in the Decorated Gothic style. As

Opposite: The church was built during the period 1107–21 on the standard plan of the greatest Norman and European churches: aisled nave, transepts, crossing tower and elaborate chancel with radiating chapels (right).

Below: The crossing tower is 'probably the largest and finest Romanesque tower in England'. Typically, all the surfaces surrounding the bell-openings are decorated with blank arcading and other work.

a result this part of the building has little of the early Norman austerity. The chancel was given a stone-ribbed vault at the same time as the nave. The bosses have the Yorkist Plantagenet badges of the 'sun in splendour'. All is splendidly done over in gilt and glowing red and blue colours. The crossing tower was stone-vaulted at the same time, the Yorkist badge prominent within a red octagon of ribs.

Eleanor de Clare donated the seven large stained glass windows in the chancel at the same time as other

Opposite: The nave elevation is of two very different periods. Below are the typically Norman elephantine piers and then the small windows. Above them is the fine stone-ribbed roof of 1340, but it is set so low above the windows that it appears to crush what is below.

Left: At the west end the main entrance is marked by a series of giant Norman arches which rise to the full height of the building. The window is a seventeenth-century insertion.

work was also donated. It is of the highest quality from a time when English stained glass work was at its best. The photograph on page 44 shows one of the windows displaying four nobles in contemporary armour standing beneath ornate canopies. Notice the slightly swaying lines of their bodies, typical of the mid-Gothic love of sinuosity. The rich greens and reds are particularly attractive as is the use of much silvery white glass.

The 'magnificent series of monuments which are the crowning part of this [eastern] part of the church are second only to those at Westminster [Abbey]'. There are three chantry chapels constructed for priests to say masses in perpetuity for the salvation of the builders' souls. They are of the stone-cage type, miniature buildings within a building. The one shown on page 43 is that erected for Richard Beauchamp, Earl of Warwick, who died in 1421, by his wife Isabel. It is a delicately complex structure that appears as one from the outside but is of two separate storeys within. The lower storey has a panelled base with figures of angels carrying heraldic family shields. Above is an open screen supporting a fan vault within. There are intricately carved canopies facing the chancel at the top of the chapel.

Of equal interest, but very different in character and purpose, is the monument to a fourteenth-century monk, possibly an abbot or a prior. His cadaver is shown in an open shroud lying on a marble slab. A mouse, a frog and a beetle crawl over the decaying body. Above him is a profusely decorated ogee arch with tracery of the period. Compared with the Beauchamp chantry, which is as much a show of wealth as of piety, this is a macabre *memento mori*, emphasising the transience and ultimate end of the physical body, something from which those from the Middle Ages did not shrink.

On 4 May 1471 the abbey was a spectator to a key event in English medieval history when the Battle of Tewkesbury was fought nearby, bringing a temporary

Top, right: The chancel was rebuilt in the early fourteenth century by the noble de Clare and Despenser families. It has a gorgeously colourful and gilded roof with a complex pattern of ribs.

Bottom, right: The ceiling of the crossing tower had the Yorkist badge of 'the sun in splendour' added after 1471, when the forces of the Yorkist Edward IV defeated those of the Lancastrian Henry VI at the edge of the town.

Opposite: The Beauchamp chantry chapel in the chancel. The beautifully ornate stone cage-like structure was built for priests to say mass for the soul of Richard Beauchamp, Earl of Warwick, who died in 1421. It is one of three in the chancel.

Opposite: A series of windows in
the chancel made during 1340–44
was also donated by the de
Clares and Despensers. This one
shows nobility connected with
the abbey. Left to Right: Richard
Fitzhamon, founder of the abbey,
Hugh Despenser, Gilbert de Clare
and Robert Consul, son-in-law of
Robert Fitzhamon who completed
the church in 1121. They are
shown as armed knights under
elaborate canopies. The glowing
colours, especially the green,
are regarded as the best work
of the period.

halt to the long, drawn-out Wars of the Roses which
in one form or another plagued the middle years of
the fifteenth century. On that day the future Edward IV
and his two brothers led the Yorkist army that defeated
the army of the Lancastrian Henry VI led by the latter's
son Edward, Prince of Wales. Margaret of Anjou,
Henry's queen, watched the battle from the abbey's
tower as the Lancastrians were routed. Henry's son was
killed and many of the defeated fled into the church for
sanctuary but to no avail. The Prince of Wales was later
buried in the chancel. Henry VI was murdered a few
days later in London.

Above: There is a grim *memento mori* at the east end in the form
of a monument for a mid-fifteenth-century monk. It shows his
cadaver in an open shroud with a mouse, frog and beetle crawling
over it. The traceried arch above is a common type of medieval
superstructure.

Just two generations later, the abbey was to see the
arrival of another, albeit smaller, army when Henry
VIII's commissioners arrived to expel the monks, take
away any of the abbey's treasures that could be sold,
and confiscate its estates. This place has seen both the
rough and the smooth of English history.

4

THE ABBEY CHURCH OF OUR LORD, ST MARY AND ST GERMAIN, SELBY, NORTH YORKSHIRE

A Towering Presence in a Town Market Place

SELBY IS A SMALL TOWN about ten miles south of York on the River Ouse. A central market place and a variety of light industries make for a busy centre. It was long associated with one of the largest coalfields in England.

A Benedictine abbey was founded here in 1069, a witness to the speed with which the Normans reached the north of England only three years after the Conquest. The church was built in 1097–1123 under Abbot Hugh de Lacey. Putting aside Westminster Abbey, which is in a class of its own, Selby Abbey might be placed in the top four surviving non-cathedral monastic churches alongside Tewkesbury, Gloucestershire (see chapter 3), Romsey and Christchurch, Hampshire. The monastery, like all others, was dissolved by Henry VIII in the 1530s. The domestic buildings have disappeared entirely, pillaged for their stone, but the church has survived in its entirety. It was used as a parish church by the people but did not, as some others did, pass immediately into full parochial use. It became almost derelict until the early seventeenth century, when its fortunes revived, but it was badly treated by the soldiers of Oliver Cromwell's Puritan army later in the century. The eighteenth century was not always a good period for the maintenance of old churches either, so it is only since the nineteenth century that proper care has been taken of buildings such as this.

The church presides over one end of a large rectangular market place in the manner of major

churches in mainland Europe. It is unusual in England, where even the large town churches contrive to hide themselves in narrow streets, revealing their presence only by their spires or towers. Although the west entrance front facing the market is separated from it by only a few yards there are ample grounds to the south and particularly the north, where there is effectively a small park, making it both a part of the bustle of the town and a place of peace and seclusion.

The prominence of the church seen from the market place is accentuated by the pure whiteness of the stone, particularly brilliant in sunlight. At first sight it might appear to be Portland Stone, a limestone from the Dorset coast first popularised by Sir Christopher Wren in his rebuilding of St Paul's Cathedral and the parish churches of the City of London after the Great Fire in 1666 (see chapter 14). Even if the stone were known in the twelfth century, the task of transporting vast quantities so far north would have been impossible then. The stone at Selby, like Portland Stone, is a fine-grained limestone, the pure white colour of both being due to the absence of the iron oxides that colour most of the other English limestones from a pale cream to a deep honey colour. The abbey's stone comes from a narrow geological formation running north–south through Yorkshire between the Pennines and the east coast. The principal quarries are at Tadcaster between York and Selby. Due to the stone containing an unusually high percentage of magnesium carbonate

Opposite: The twin-towered west front is typically Norman, but everything above the ground stage was later rebuilt at various times from the thirteenth to the nineteenth century.

within the predominant calcium carbonate, it is known as magnesian limestone. Like Portland Stone it has weathered well in the polluted atmospheres of modern cities and towns. It has been used widely on buildings in the area, from the magnificent York Minster to humble village cottages.

The abbey church consists of a nave and aisles fronted at the west end by twin towers, north and south transepts and a crossing tower taller than the west towers. Further east there is a long chancel with its own aisles. The plan is a classic Romanesque one, which by 1000 was standard throughout Europe in all the greater churches. It vies with the largest and grandest cathedrals in England. That it should have survived Henry VIII's dissolution and the despoliation

and neglect of later times is remarkably fortunate. The west entrance front gives an indication of its Norman origins only at the ground stage. The central portal is typically Norman, built up of a series of round-headed arches, each within the other, receding into the thickness of the wall. Although the Normans generally made a great effort in the decoration of their doorways, here the arches have only the ubiquitous Norman zig-zag ornament with a minimum of other types. Given the size of the church this is relatively unambitious by the standards of the time. The tiny church at Kilpeck (see chapter 2) is, by comparison, much more impressive in its wealth of imaginative figure carvings. The monks, as opposed to a Norman Marcher Lord, may have deliberately avoided such individualism.

Above: The Norman doorway has five 'orders' of round-headed arches receding into the thickness of the wall. They are covered overall with zig-zag decoration.

Below: The chancel is an entirely Gothic rebuilding of the Norman one. The aisle windows are in the Geometrical Decorated style. The clerestory windows above are of the later Flowing Decorated style with sinuous tracery.

Opposite: The former Benedictine abbey church overlooks a large, busy market place. There are spacious grounds on the other sides.

There are Norman windows to the left and right of the door, which are very much smaller than all the later Gothic insertions. They give an idea of how dark a large Norman church must have been originally. Much of the work above the ground stage is Early English Gothic, distinguishable by its tall, narrow, lancet windows and blank wall arcading. The huge central window is an even later Perpendicular Gothic insertion, while the

two towers are from a nineteenth-century restoration. This evolutionary mix over a period of 800 years is entirely typical of English churches.

Immediately inside the main entrance at the west end of the nave the full impact of great Norman architecture hits the visitor. It is good practice in a place like this to sit and take it in for a few minutes. The impact is one of height, overpowering heaviness and grave

Left: The Norman crossing tower and south transept were substantially rebuilt after a fire in 1906.

Opposite: The nave seen in evening sunlight from the west door. The power of the Norman architecture doubtless reflects the twin powers of the Norman state and church.

solemnity. There are few decorative details to lighten the effect. The elevation is in three stages, again the classic Romanesque ideal. The ground stage is an arcade of wide arches supported by piers of complex cross-section. Above this is a gallery based on the same plan as the arcade below. Despite its name it was not designed to accommodate a congregation as were the side galleries of eighteenth-century churches. Its function is two-fold. The floor of the gallery is the roof of the aisle below, which then links it to the outer wall and provides stability to the entire structure. The galleries in large Romanesque churches such as Selby are also important aesthetically, providing vertical articulation and increased visual interest. At Selby the piers supporting the gallery arches consist of a central core surrounded by completely detached shafts, another example of articulation for aesthetic purposes. The windows are in the third, highest stage, the clerestory or 'clear-storey'. This could have been a simple two-dimensional plane, but it is made three dimensional by a low stone gallery, or passageway, running in front so everywhere there is something to engage the eye.

The nave is fascinatingly complex and worthy of much attention from the visitor. Building, as always in a medieval church, progressed from east (the chancel) to west and each bay of the nave introduces new features as the decades of work proceeded –

some minor, some more important. At the west end the gallery arches are actually pointed, presaging the coming Gothic style of the late twelfth century. The Norman chancel was rebuilt in the Decorated Gothic style (c.1280–1340), to form a sizeable church in its own right. It has already been said that most of the Norman windows were replaced in many parts of the church. The aisle and clerestory windows have Decorated tracery. The huge windows of the transept fronts are fourteenth-century Decorated on the south side and fifteenth-century Perpendicular on the north. Above all else, however, it is the Norman work at Selby that sticks in the memory. Raoul Glaber, a monk of Cluny in France, wrote in 1003:

> Therefore, after the above mentioned year of the millennium, now about three years past, there occurred throughout the world, especially in Italy and Gaul a rebuilding of church basilicas. Each Christian people strove against each other to erect nobler ones. It was if the whole earth, having cast off the old by shaking itself, were clothing itself everywhere in the white robe of the Church.

This clothing of the earth with noble Romanesque churches was to continue throughout that century and nowhere more so than in Norman England.

Opposite: The three-stage elevation of the nave – arcade, gallery and clerestory – is typical of all great churches built during the medieval period. As building progressed from east to west over several decades, the Norman round arches of the arcade were overtaken by the pointed Gothic arches of the gallery and clerestory.

THE MIDDLE AGES, 1200–1500

The Gothic Style: Churches with a New Spirit

In northern France in the early twelfth century a number of architectural features that had already been used in various places in Europe were brought together in one building with a dramatic effect to create the Gothic style. It is a style associated above all else with the pointed arch as opposed to the round arch of the Norman Romanesque style. It may be asked how the simple change in the shape of an arch created a new 'style'. In itself it did not. Nonetheless, the change alone was significant. Once the distance between the two columns supporting a round arch are fixed, the height to which the arch rises is also

fixed. Pointed arches, on the other hand, can be struck with any degree of acuteness, from moderate to extreme. The pointed arches, which are used everywhere in Gothic churches, from the arcades that support the main structure to the doors, windows and decorative features, give the buildings an upward, heaven-pointing character in contrast to the earth-bound Romanesque. The pointed arch, however, has a more fundamental role in the construction of a building. It gives more flexibility to the design and construction of the important upper parts, especially the heavier stone roofs. The pointed arch enables the

The donors of medieval stained glass windows – aristocrats or tradesmen – often liked to record their portraits and generosity for posterity in 'donor panels' at the bases of the windows. This example shows male and female members of the Martyn family at St Neots, Cornwall.

Elizabeta nat Talbot Elizabeta nat Tilney

Ducissa Norfoltia ur Thome howard

At Long Melford, Suffolk, a late-fifteenth-century window shows the Duchess of Norfolk (left) and the Countess of Surrey. The former is said to be the model for John Tenniel's illustration of the duchess in *Alice in Wonderland*.

provided with small windows. Thus the Gothic style is associated with light in two senses of the word – light as opposed to heavy and light as opposed to dark. It is not the physical features but the bringing together of these features – the pointed arch, a ribbed form of roofing and various types of buttresses – that created a startling new spirit of *zeitgeist* which is the essential characteristic of a new 'style'.

The rebuilding of the east end of the Norman cathedral at Canterbury after a fire in 1180 heralded the arrival of the Gothic style in England under the direction of the Frenchman William of Sens. It caught the English imagination and became the only architectural style used here until the sixteenth century. Its popularity waned in the seventeenth and eighteenth centuries, although it was never completely abandoned, and it was again revived by a number of passionate advocates in the early nineteenth century from when it continued to be used in one form or another into modern times.

The architect and architectural historian Thomas Rickman (1776–1841) was the first to identify and give names to three phases in English Gothic building history. It is a classification that has proved continuously useful to both academics and a wider public ever since. The dates given below are only approximate guides:

Early English Gothic: 1180–1250
Decorated Gothic (in two sub-periods): 1250–1350
Perpendicular Gothic: 1350–1600

The styles are surprisingly easy to recognise by their different window designs. Early English has narrow lancets with simple pointed heads. Decorated has much wider structures made up of multiple lights with stone 'tracery' in the heads with regular circular patterns (Geometrical Decorated) or the later complex sinuous patterns (Flowing or Curvilinear Decorated). Perpendicular is characterised by tracery dominated by parallel vertical lines that give the style its name. Constantly changing preferences during the later Middle Ages do mean that any one of these types of windows may have been inserted into a much older building or may have been imitated in a more modern building. This limits the conclusions that can be drawn on the basis of window design alone.

construction of ribs, which can carry the heavy weight of a roof to selected points on the side walls that can be buttressed at these points. Walls can then be made thinner, with greater areas opened up to glass. In a Romanesque building the heavy weight of the upper parts is carried continuously along the length of thick walls, which for safety's sake could only be

5
ST MARY, WEST WALTON, NORFOLK

The Finest of Early English Gothic

THE SMALL VILLAGE OF WEST Walton is a few miles south-west of Kings Lynn in the fenlands of north-west Norfolk, adjacent to the Lincolnshire Fens. To the visitor the region can have an empty, melancholic atmosphere. The large dykes that criss-cross the flat landscape and the smaller ditches that border most of the fields show that immense effort has been necessary to keep the land drained and workable over the centuries. The Norfolk Fens have an extraordinary number of fine churches, probably more per square mile than any other place in England, although the reason for this is not clear. The churches span the centuries, from twelfth-century Norman to late medieval, and so they cannot be ascribed to the prosperity of any particular time, like the 'Wool Churches' of Somerset or the Cotswolds.

The village houses are grouped around the junction of several minor roads about a mile from the Kings Lynn–Wisbech road. It is not an especially picturesque village by the standards of others in Norfolk. However, the characteristically East Anglian picture sign at the entrance to the village shows that the villagers are proud of having one piece of architecture of national importance in their midst – the great detached bell tower of their parish church. Their church of St Mary is an outstanding example of the first period of Gothic architecture in England (*c.*1180–1250), which is known as Early English.

Opposite: The detached bell tower at the entrance to the churchyard is a rarity in England. Proudly tall and broad, it displays many Early English Gothic structural and decorative features.

Left: The tower seen from the west end of the church. The archways below act as entrances to the churchyard.

In its simplest expression, the Early English style can be calm, cool and rather unexciting. Arches outside and inside have simple chamfers, and piers are round or octagonal with insignificant capitals. When the necessary money was available, the imagination and skill of the best masons could transform this into something exuberantly ornate. The money and skill were available at such Early English cathedrals as Salisbury and Wells. They were also clearly available at West Walton, where the church and tower have all the external, structural and decorative features of the Early English style at its most sumptuous.

The church was built in the 1240s, towards the end of the Early English period. The rare feature of a detached bell tower was built a few years after the body of the church was complete, although it was undoubtedly planned from the start. It stands about 30 yards south of the church at the entrance to the churchyard. Detached bell towers derive from the popular Italian *campanili* of the eleventh and twelfth centuries. There are only about 50 in England, many of them along the Welsh border, where they have a defensive character. The tower and the church behind it are built of silver-grey Jurassic limestone from Barnack near Peterborough. During the Middle Ages, this was a source of good building stone for East Anglia, which had little good stone of its own. Barnack stone is hard enough to withstand the weather but soft enough for the elaborate carving that was

The village sign is typically East Anglian. The people clearly identify themselves with the great mid-thirteenth-century tower of their parish church. Sheep were the basis of much of the prosperity of medieval Norfolk.

When seen from inside the churchyard the lack of an attached bell tower gives the church a rather barn-like appearance.

58

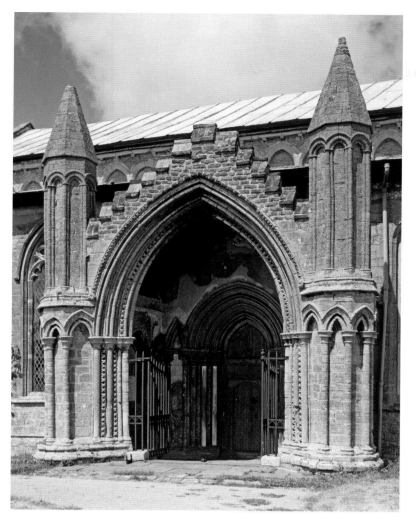

The two doorways have a sumptuousness not often seen in parish churches.

Left: The south porch and doorway are embellished everywhere with panelling and deeply undercut mouldings.

Right: The west doorway has twin doors separated by a central column, a feature normally found only in cathedrals and abbey churches.

required at West Walton. The tower is an impressive, powerful, three-stage structure that is broad as well as tall. The ground stage has open arches on all four sides acting as entrances into the churchyard as though it were a gatehouse as well as a belfry. The arches have gabled niches to the left and right. In the stage above there are three tall, narrow lancets with subsidiary side-shafts. Windows or unglazed openings like this are characteristic of the Early English period and are an easy way to recognise the style. The bell-stage has lancets too, but here they are twinned under a super arch. The massive polygonal buttresses that conceal the corners of the tower have more blank arcading of the lancet type. The decorated parapet and four corner pinnacles were added in the fifteenth century. The whole composition is a masterpiece of proportion and design.

The reason for building a detached bell tower at West Walton is probably technical rather than defensive or aesthetic. The marshy subsoil of the fens provides a poor foundation for such a heavy structure as this. Had an attached tower collapsed it might have brought much of the church to the ground with it. A similar thing was done at nearby Terrington St Clement, although there the tower is only a few yards from the church. The cost of the upkeep of this great structure is too large for a small community and it is now in the care of the Churches Conservation Trust.

Lacking an attached tower the church behind inevitably has a rather barn-like appearance. The chancel is almost as long as the nave, as though there were a resident college of priests who would require the space for the daily offices. None of the windows in the nave or chancel is original, reflecting the desire during the Decorated and Perpendicular periods for ever more light. The church has two very ornate original doorways. The main south door for everyday use has a deep stone porch. The steeply pointed front arch has multiple roll mouldings. To the left and right are clasping polygonal buttresses with blank arcading of the type seen in the tower. The brickwork above is Tudor. The second entrance at the west end would have been used for special occasions such as the Easter

ceremonies. It has two doorways with twin arches separated by a central column known as a trumeau. The whole is set within a round outer arch of the type normally seen only in cathedrals and abbey churches.

The two doorways are a suitable introduction to the equally spectacular interior, which is distinguished principally by the magnificent arcade between nave and aisles. The arches rise from circular piers, each surrounded by a ring of completely detached shafts of dark Purbeck marble. This shelly limestone (it is not a true marble in the geological sense) from the Dorset coast near Swanage was a very popular decorative stone in the thirteenth century and was used in cathedrals and abbeys all over England. The fact that the stone and its transport costs could be afforded emphasises the wealth available at West Walton. The piers and the shafts have 'stiff-leaf' decoration, which is a form of three-leafed foliage based on the acanthus leaf. In the first years of the Early English period it was cut in low relief. Here in the later years of the period it was deeply undercut and became alive with movement as though blowing in a breeze from the open south and west doors. The arches above have again deeply undercut roll mouldings which produce a rippling effect beloved of more skilled Gothic masons. It can be seen to even greater effect at the east end of the nave where it meets the chancel. Within the latter, the walls have the same blank arcading as in the tower, south porch and elsewhere. It was the aim of Gothic masons to leave as little blank wall as possible.

The church is now much larger than needed for the present-day congregations, and a few rows of chairs at the front of the nave are sufficient. The remainder of the nave, consequently, has the sense of spaciousness that it would have had originally. The floor of large irregular slabs of stone contributes to the atmosphere. All this indicates another church that escaped Victorian restoration when encaustic tiles would have been inserted beneath pine benches. This was a favourite church of John Piper (1902–93), landscape and architectural painter, stained glass artist and travelling companion of John Betjeman. It is easy to understand why.

Opposite: The splendid nave arcade. The piers have detached subsidiary shafts of dark Purbeck marble from the Dorset coast and stiff-leaf capitals.

Above, left: Nave pier detail. The stiff-leaf foliage is an Early English leitmotif. The leaves, cut by a master carver, appear to be blowing in the wind.

Left: The side walls of the chancel have the same blank arcading seen elsewhere on tower and church.

6

THE MINSTER, BEVERLEY, EAST YORKSHIRE

A Parish Church Rivalled by Few Others

BEVERLEY IS ONE OF MANY ancient market towns that have succeeded in combining the needs and style of modern life with the beauty of their historic buildings and the atmosphere of the past that those create. The walls of the medieval town have been retained only in the tall North Bar, or gateway, of 1409, whose brickwork is attractively mellow. The houses start with a few from the seventeenth century and then a wealth of others from the early to late eighteenth century. Many of the moderately sized ones lining Beverley's Wednesday Market and Saturday Market and other streets have had their ground floors converted into shops. Much grander houses hide themselves away in the narrow lanes that lie behind. Only a few Victorian and twentieth-century buildings intrude in the historic centre.

Opposite: The minster field provides a view of almost the full length of one of the largest parish churches in England. The two pairs of transepts (right) and the stately twin towers at the west end are exceptional even by cathedral standards. The east end of the building was begun c.1230, but breaks in construction meant that the west end was not completed until c.1450.

It is not unusual for an old town to have two or more medieval churches within a short distance of each other: townsfolk of the Middle Ages did not hold back when it came to churches. What *is* unique is for a town to have two of the size and magnificence of those at Beverley. St Mary's church at the north end of the town is very grand by any standards. It has Norman origins but belongs mainly to the fourteenth and fifteenth centuries. In almost any place it would be the principal focus of architectural attention by far. However, at the south end of the town, just a few hundred yards away, the second church, generally known as the Minster, transports us to another realm: the realm of cathedral-like grandeur,

overpowering in its size and beauty. Indeed it outranks several English cathedrals in these respects. As a parish church it is rivalled by only some six others, or even fewer if one excludes the former monastic churches (see chapters 3 and 4).

The existence of a minster at Beverley goes back to St John of Beverley, who founded the original church here *c.*690 at a time when Northumbria was the pre-eminent Saxon kingdom, and was already at this early date committed to Christianity. John became bishop of Hexham, then of York. He retired to Beverley and is buried here. The word 'minster' derives from the Latin *monasterium* via the German *münster*. It has developed a number of meanings over the centuries. Literally translated it means a monastery or monastery church. The name was also given to cathedrals, such as York, Ripon and Southwell, that were not combined with a monastery and ruled over by an abbot-bishop. In Saxon and later times a minster could also denote a collegiate church staffed by a team of priests who were not necessarily monks. Today we might think of the team ministries that have been established in cities and rural areas to serve a group of parish churches. John's minster was sacked by the Vikings but refounded *c.*935 by King Athelstan as a collegiate establishment. Whatever structure was in existence at the time of the Conquest was replaced by the Normans. Nothing but the font of that church survives. The minster we have today was established in 1230 and dedicated to St John and St Martin.

The minster is extremely fortunate in its immediate surroundings. On the north, east and west sides the houses bordering narrow streets come within a few yards of the church. This is no bad thing – it ties the building to the people it serves. However, on the south side there is a small churchyard and beyond that an extensive meadow owned by the minster. From there visitors can take in the splendid view of the entire length of the church (a special boon to church photographers).

From its beginning in 1230 work proceeded from east to west in the traditional medieval way, as the chancel – the most important part of a church – was required first. Due to a considerable pause midway through construction the building was not finally completed at the west end for another 200 years. The plan is a chancel with aisles, two sets of transepts (a feature found only in the greater cathedrals) and an aisled nave. There is a low crossing tower and two west towers which combine monumentally with slender elegance. The eastern half of the church is in the Early English Gothic style. The arches here are sharply pointed and there is prolific use of very dark Purbeck marble (a limestone from the Dorset coast) in subsidiary shafts. The capitals of piers in the main and subsidiary structures have the characteristic stiff leaf of the period, lush foliage based on acanthus leaves. These features are incorporated in the beautiful double staircase leading up to the former chapter house which has disappeared. By the time the nave was reached

Opposite: The east end was started in the thirteenth century when the Early English Gothic style was created. The double staircase from the north chancel aisle into a former chapter house is an exquisite example of the work done when finance was available. The black Purbeck marble shafts and sharply pointed trefoils are distinctively Early English.

Left: The canopy of the tomb of Lady Eleanor Percy (died 1328) illustrates how Decorated Gothic acquired its name. The arches, buttresses and pinnacles are filled with tiny heads of Christ, the Virgin Mary, angels, saints and knights.

the early Gothic style had developed into Decorated, but in a spirit of conservatism the masons largely retained the earlier style except for the windows, now much enlarged with sinuous tracery in the heads. Throughout the building the elevation is in three stages. The arcade below has piers with moulded shafts, which give the whole building a rippling effect in the Gothic way. Above the arcade is a triforum, or narrow wall passage, with its own arcading towards the nave. This is a smaller version of the massive galleries seen in the greater Norman churches (see chapters 3 and 4). The upper stage is the clerestory of windows. The roofs are stone-vaulted throughout as one would expect in a building of this distinction. The west front brings us to the first half of the fifteenth century. The twin towers, the main west doorway and the window tracery all have a proliferation of the vertical lines in the panelling and tracery that give Perpendicular Gothic its name.

It is only possible to describe a few of the furnishings. Evidence of the earlier Saxon and Norman churches is limited but interesting. In the choir there is a Saxon stone seat, or throne, a squat sturdy structure with back and arms of the same height, completely unadorned. A naïve oil painting from the late fifteenth century recalls the Saxon period, with portraits of

Opposite: Four of a large number of fourteenth-century musicians carved along the outer wall of the north aisle. Clockwise from top left: medieval versions of drums, bagpipes, guitar and violin.

Above: The 'Frith Stone', a Saxon tub chair perhaps from the time of St John of Beverley, who founded the first minster c.690.

Right: A rustic late-fifteenth-century painting of St John of Beverley and King Athelstan, who refounded the minster c.935 after Viking raids.

Left: The choir stalls of 1520 have intricate canopies darkened with age.

Bottom: The large, black marble Norman font is dwarfed by the suspended 1713 font cover, which was designed by Nicholas Hawksmoor or his school.

St John of Beverley and King Athelstan. From the Norman church there is a font in the south aisle, a heavy circular tub with fluted sides. It is made of dark Frosterley marble, a local stone resembling Purbeck. The font itself is quite overwhelmed by the huge 1713 font cover decorated with eight carved scrolls. Raised and lowered by a pulley, it is 'a magnificent piece of metropolitan quality'.

Those involved in the minster in the centuries after it was built clearly had a particular love of music. There are portraits of musicians carved in stone in many places – on capitals, bosses and hood stops. The most interesting and fortunately the easiest to study is a long line of musicians playing an intriguing variety of instruments carved along the north aisle wall. The instruments include medieval versions of the modern violin, guitar, flute and bagpipes.

There are several interesting monuments spanning 500 years. The most spectacular is the Percy Tomb, 'the most splendid of all British Decorated Gothic Monuments'. The Percy family, as Earls of Northumberland, were powerful in this part of England. The tomb, although not inscribed, is probably that of Lady Eleanor Percy who died in 1328.

Left: The west door, by Nicholas Hawksmoor or his school, is carved with figures of the four Evangelists and their symbols.

Right: Monument to Major-General B. Foord Bowes (died 1812). The angel writes 'Pro Patriae' in a book. Military objects include cannons and cannon balls.

The structure around and above the tomb chest rises to some 20 feet. It is a typical Decorated masterpiece crowded with arches, gables, buttresses and pinnacles. These are embellished with innumerable small carvings of angels and saints as well as heraldry. On the apex of all this a figure of Christ holds the deceased's soul in a napkin.

In the choir there is a complete set of stalls made for the priests of the college in 1520. They have tall, intricately carved oak canopies that have aged to almost black.

Apart from the font cover the eighteenth century's contribution to woodwork is the west doors. They are of the same date and school of craftsmanship and were possibly designed by Nicholas Hawksmoor. The inner side of the door has figures of the four evangelists and *putti* representing the four seasons.

In places like this the work of the twentieth and twenty-first centuries has been, and continues to be, centred on the enormous responsibility of repair and conservation. Additions to the structure are of course no longer necessary in our own time,

but present-day church people like to continue the centuries-old tradition by making their own mark. The most appropriate way of doing this is in the form of contemporary works of art. Before the Reformation cathedrals and great churches nearly always had shrines to local saints which attracted large numbers of pilgrims. It has become common to recreate these with modern versions to encourage a spirit of prayerfulness. In the retrochoir at Beverley the Shrine of St John of Beverley was among the most popular in England before it was destroyed on the orders of Henry VIII. In more modern times, artist Helen Whittaker was commissioned to make a bronze sculpture to remind people of the origins of the minster. Entitled *Pilgrims*, it captures the spirit of a medieval pilgrimage with a group of people clutching their staffs, backs bent after a long journey (see page 187).

Modern pilgrims do not require the same commitment and effort but they do leave with the same thrill of the sublime after visiting and worshipping at Beverley Minster.

7

ST MARY, RIPPLE, WORCESTERSHIRE

A Village Woodcarver Records the Medieval Country Year

THE PARISH CHURCH IS TUCKED away in a secluded corner of a quiet village about four miles north of Tewkesbury. The large churchyard is ringed by trees on two sides, which screen it from the nearby houses, while the third side looks out onto open fields. The fourth side overlooks at a distance the large former rectory of 1726, a brick building with stone dressings in the neat Classical style of the time. The rectory cellars, however, have thirteenth-century stonework, perhaps part of an early clergy house. The residence is surrounded by ample lawns, trees and shrubberies and could have accommodated a family of eight with indoor servants. Jane Austen would have been at home in such a comfortable clerical world.

North-west view of the church. Originally Norman, it was extended several times during the Middle Ages.

The handsome former rectory built near the church in 1726 is redolent of a long-gone age of wealthy and leisured Church of England clergymen.

Overleaf: The 12 labours of the months, showing medieval peasants at work, are carved into the undersides of the choir stall seats.

Needless to say Ripple is now grouped with four other churches in a united benefice.

The church consists of a nave with aisles, and north and south transepts with a crossing tower. It is an impressively large building for such a remote place. It is built of the red sandstone that underlies much of the west midland country of England. The church dates from c.1180, from which time a number of late-Norman details remain, giving way to early Gothic work. The chancel was rebuilt in the late thirteenth century. The transepts were used as chantry chapels during the period c.1320–1510. The upper part of the tower is late Gothic as is the north porch. The early eighteenth century gave the tower a balustrade and a second storey to the porch. The nineteenth century provided stained glass by C. E. Kempe. The twentieth century has been much concerned with extensive conservation work. So all the centuries have added to and cared for this church in the usual English way.

The chancel has a rare set of furnishings of outstanding human interest. There was a set of 16 choir stalls. However, today only 12 remain – six on either side. The missing four originally faced the altar at the entrance to the chancel. The existence of the choir stalls presupposes a number of clergy – the only people with access to a chancel in the Middle Ages. Furthermore, only a monastery or collegiate church would have a staff of 16 priests. The presence of the Ripple choir stalls may be connected with the non-monastic Augustinian canons who staffed the chantry chapels in the transepts.

Choir stalls consisted of tip-up seats separated by armrests. The seats were provided with ledges on their undersides so that when the monks were standing with the seats tipped back there was a support that enabled them to adopt in effect a semi-sitting position without it being obvious. It was traditional for the undersides of the seats to be carved and these carvings took a wide variety of forms. There were sacred subjects and symbols and heraldic arms. Animal subjects could display black humour, such as a group of mice hanging a cat. Violence was not eschewed, as wives beat husbands with kitchen implements or schoolmasters birched their pupils. Strangely in such places there were digs at church life, such as a fox preaching to a group of geese. One of the most interesting subjects was the labours of the months. This was a set of carvings showing the various jobs that peasants had to carry out in the fields and in their houses in each of the 12 months of the year. The Ripple set is carved in a 'delightfully lively manner' with much intriguing detail, probably in the fifteenth century by a local man. These vignettes are a striking example of the way in which the everyday life of people was brought into parish churches (see Introduction). The grand monuments tell us something about the lives of the great people, and the minor monuments tell us about the middle classes. Here, for a change, we learn something about the lives of the little people.

January. Collecting large tree branches for firewood.

February. Splitting wood to make fences.

March. Sowing seeds from a basket. A horse pulls a harrow that covers the seeds with soil.

April. Scaring birds away from the growing seeds with noise-making devices.

May. Not a labour of the month but the image of the Virgin Mary, to whom this month is dedicated. She represents the blessing of the fields and crops at Rogationtide.

June. A man on a horse goes hawking. (The bird has broken off.)

July. Two men with staves guard a bakery with oven door above and a loaf of bread below.

August. A man with a sickle and a woman with a crook reaping.

September. Collecting corn for malting.

October. Beating down acorns for pigs.

November. Killing a pig to be salted for winter.

December. Alongside a fire with a cooking pot a man helps a woman with her spinning.

8
HOLY TRINITY, BLYTHBURGH, SUFFOLK

A Memorable Combination of Grandeur and Charm

THE QUIET VILLAGE OF BLYTHBURGH lies on the little river Blyth which runs into the North Sea near Southwold about four miles to the east. Despite being so far inland, it was a port of some significance in the late Middle Ages, when the river banks here were lined with wharves for fishing boats and ships trading with the continent. However, by 1500 trade was in decline as the shallow river could

Late medieval architecture of 1450–1500 on a grand scale in a small village. The two long regular lines of windows in the aisles and upper nave give the exterior an impressive unity.

At its east end (left) the church adjoins the village street, but on the other three sides it adjoins the salt marshes of the tidal River Blyth. Although three miles from the sea Blythburgh was once a busy port.

not take ships of increasing draught. Today only small pleasure craft make their way up and down the river and the village is a quieter place. The tidal river flowing through the flat landscape has created salt marshes all around, giving places to walk and enjoy wildlife.

It is well known that Suffolk and neighbouring Norfolk are particularly rich in medieval churches, and there are more to the square mile than in any other English county. Most of the original churches were Norman but the wealth of the area in the fourteenth and fifteenth centuries, which derived from the wool trade, led to widespread rebuilding as it did in Somerset, Gloucestershire and elsewhere. Wealth and piety combined to give rise to huge churches in the smallest villages, churches built for the glory of God rather than simply to accommodate people.

The immediate surroundings of Blythburgh church are ideal. The village comes up close to the east end,

making it possible for most people to walk to services and providing a sense of togetherness between building and people. However, on the north, south and west sides the church and churchyard are open to the river and the marshes, providing a sense of otherness in the peace of nature below vast skies. The present church was built in 1440–60 in a single campaign to replace an earlier one. As a result it is all of a piece architecturally. From the south-east entrance to the churchyard there is an unobstructed view of its entire length, where the special character of late-medieval East Anglian churches is strikingly displayed. In an area short of good building stone, limestone imported from Lincolnshire and elsewhere was combined with the extensive use of the flint that was available in the fields as small irregularly shaped pieces on or just below the surface. This strangest of stones is a form of silica, chemically the same as sandstone in an

Opposite: The priest's door into the chancel is marked by a miniature flying buttress. Several different types of flint stonework can be seen.

The aisle parapet is pierced by quatrefoils and the buttresses are topped by animals; this one is a bear.

An inscription in flint flushwork below the chancel east window has the letters 'ANJBST MSAHR'. They can be taken to be the first letters of a Latin dedication that in translation reads: 'In the name of the Blessed Jesus, the Holy Trinity [and] in honour of Holy Mary, Anne and Katherine the church was rebuilt'.

amorphous physical form, noted for its hardness and hence resistance to cutting and shaping. Nonetheless, the medieval masons, carrying on a tradition that goes back to the stone and bronze ages, learnt how to adapt it to their purposes. Pieces of many shades, ranging from pure white through mid-brown to jet black, occur together in the ground and will be seen together in the same building to pleasing effect. Even at a distance the walls of Blythburgh church are recognisable by this mottled appearance. Only at the corners, on decorative parapets and on the jambs and tracery of the windows was it necessary to use the silver-grey limestone.

In terms of architecture the fourteenth and fifteenth centuries were the period of Perpendicular Gothic, which favoured huge windows that made walls more glass than stone so that in a large church the effect is almost that of a glasshouse. There is a curious parallel in spirit, if not in artistic forms, with the large, ultra-modern commercial buildings, with their vast expanses of plate glass, erected in city centres today. At the Blythburgh churchyard gate the eye is immediately caught by the two long lines of closely spaced windows: the larger windows of the aisle, separated by deep buttresses, and the smaller ones in the clerestory above, two for every one below, are all arranged with the regularity of two ranks of soldiers. The west tower is rather too low and too narrow in relation to the body of the church. It belongs to the predecessor of the present church which was evidently a humbler building.

A close approach to the church shows the variety of ways the masons used flint in this and other churches. There is plain unworked flint in the older tower, which is totally irregular in size and shape and of necessity placed in position with much mortar. In the aisles and chancel there is advancing refinement. Here knapped flint, produced by splitting the pieces with a blow from a sharp tool and placing the flat surfaces thus produced outwards in the walls, is used. This gives a smoother, less rustic appearance. In the more visible positions, such as the front of the two-storey south porch, the knapped flint is further regularised as the pieces are squared off by chipping. These knapped and squared flints could then, if desired, be used to produce a chequered, chess board effect by placing black and white pieces alternately. The most skilled flint craftsmen could employ the most difficult technique of all. Flushwork consists of splitting and shaping pieces of white flint into curved pieces to create lettering and then setting

them into black pieces to compose inscriptions. There is an excellent example in the east wall below the chancel window, where there are the initial letters of a Latin dedication: 'Ad Honorem Jesu Beati Sanctae Trinitas Mariae [et] Sanctae Annae Hic Reconstructus [est]' ('To the honour of Blessed Jesus, the Holy Trinity, Mary and Saint Anne this chancel has been rebuilt' — this is a speculative translation of the lettering). An alternative interpretation sees the letters as the initials of various prominent persons in the parish at the time.

At the east end the priest's door into the chancel has its position stressed by a small flying buttress springing from the main buttress wall with the elaborate use of flint work. The parapet that runs above the aisle roof is pierced by quatrefoils containing various

Opposite: The tall and wide nave with slender, widely spaced arches, large windows and lime-washed walls has a marvellously spacious airy and bright atmosphere.

Below: A holy water stoup at the main entrance to the church. For such a Catholic item to survive the Reformation in such a prominent place is remarkable.

figures, human and animal, placed on the heads of the buttresses. There is a prominent two-storey south porch. The upper chambers could be used as a priest's room, school room or safe rooms for valuables and vestments. This one, which is accessed from inside the church, has been converted into a small chapel with good, simple contemporary furnishings. To the side of the porch doorway there is a holy water stoup. If this is a pre-Reformation holy water stoup, still found in the porches of Roman Catholic churches today, it has had a remarkable escape from the destruction of 'popish' objects, particularly as it is in such a prominent place.

It is worthwhile pausing here to appreciate the enormous amount of work – and money – that must have gone into fashioning the tons of flint in the church, not forgetting the limestone in the windows and the parapets. One remembers that Blythburgh was once a larger and wealthier place.

The nave is entered through the original fifteenth-century door. The first glimpse of the interior is as exciting as that of the exterior from the churchyard gate. The interiors of late-medieval East Anglian churches are as characteristic as their exteriors. All is spaciousness, airiness and light. The spaciousness comes from this being a tall, bright building in which there is no structural division between nave and chancel as there would have been in an early-medieval church. The slim piers supporting the wide arches that separate the nave from the aisles make these areas merge into one with a sense of air flowing around the piers. Only the front half of the nave is provided with pews and this increases the feeling of spaciousness. Neither is there

The low-pitched roof stretches without break from west to east. Pairs of angels, wings outspread, seem to flutter in an earthly heaven. Each rafter is painted overall with the symbol of Jesus, 'IHS', and floral designs.

A modern reproduction of a roof angel painted in original colours hangs above the door as if to bless worshippers as they leave.

any clutter from large, prominently placed monuments and the like. The light comes from the large clear glass windows of the aisles and the clerestory and from the plain limewashed walls.

The floor of a large building does much to define its character. In most medieval churches the Victorians provided highly coloured glazed tiles. Many are of high quality but they do not always harmonise well with ancient stonework. At Blythburgh the floors are a pleasing mixture of large stone slabs and mellowed eighteenth-century bricks (although these no doubt cause a headache for cleaners). High above, the low-pitched roof is well lit by the clerestory. At each intersection of the tie beams and the rafters are carved bosses and a pair of angels facing east and west with outstretched wings. The angels hold shields bearing the arms of the local Swillington, Ufford, and Hopton families. All the rafters are covered with the repeated Jesus monogram 'IHS'.

At ground level there are also several pieces of interesting woodwork. The choir stalls have well-carved images of the apostles and other saints. The tall rood screen separating chancel from nave is slim in the East Anglian way as opposed to the much heavier structures of Devon and Cornwall (see chapters 9 and 11). The pulpit is Jacobean. However, by far the most interesting pieces of woodwork are the carved figures at the ends of the pews. They represent people (were they recognisable local people?) engaged in the seven deadly sins – avarice, envy, gluttony, lust, pride, sloth and wrath.

Modern visitors may find them amusing, but they were meant to be salutary reminders to people who would be kneeling or sitting next to them for considerable periods each week.

The church suffered considerably under the seventeenth-century Cromwellian Commonwealth when the Puritan party was strong in the area. Squads of soldiers were sent around the churches with orders to destroy superstitious images in the form of statues, paintings and stained glass. The principal leader in Suffolk was a Captain William Dowsing, who kept a record of the items destroyed each day, clearly exulting in the destruction he was undertaking.

In the eighteenth century, the century that the Church of England 'went to sleep', the fabric suffered more than it did during the Reformation years. Through indifference the building decayed almost to the point of dereliction. Poverty in the area, however, may also have played a part. It was not until the later nineteenth century that conservation work was set in hand, fortunately without the drastic modernising common at the time. The badly decayed roof, for instance, was not ripped out and replaced but carefully raised by nine inches over its entire length. Work continues unendingly today. The result is a structurally sound building with a charming fifteenth-century interior.

In recent years the church has forged a link with the world of art. Good acoustics, recognised by Benjamin Britten, have led to the church being used for concerts at the Aldeburgh festival, and modern works of art

Above: The church has commissioned a number of high-quality works of modern art, a remarkable achievement for a small community.

Left: A modern interpretation of the Holy Trinity, to whom the church is dedicated. It occupies a niche above the main entrance that was formerly empty for 400 years after the Reformation.

Right: Madonna and Child in Byzantine style.

Opposite: Four of the remarkable fifteenth-century bench ends which depict the seven deadly sins are admonitions to parishioners who would be only a few feet away during services.

Top left: Pride. A man with fine clothes and headgear.

Top right: Gluttony. A woman clutches a full belly.

Bottom left: Sloth. A man lies abed.

Bottom right: Avarice. A woman sits on a money chest but begs for alms.

have been commissioned recently. There is an oak statue of the Virgin and Child by Peter Eugene Ball in the style of Greek icons. A niche above the south door, empty like several thousand others of its kind since the Reformation, now contains a contemporary representation of the Holy Trinity to whom the church is dedicated. Carved in stone by Nicholas Mynheer, it rightly makes no attempt to reproduce medieval or late nineteenth-century iconography.

Blythburgh is a community that respects and cares for its church and its ancient treasures and welcomes visitors to share them. Equally clear is that the church does not regard itself as a museum of village life but as a place of worship and service. It is a memorable place even among many others that are worthy of that description.

9
ST ANDREW, CULLOMPTON, DEVON

Notable in a County Famous for its Church Roofs and Screens

CULLOMPTON IS ONE OF THE easiest of the West Country's small towns to visit, as a junction of the M5 motorway is only a few yards from its eastern edge. The town prospered on the wool trade between the sixteenth and eighteenth centuries as is evidenced by the several mansions and prosperous houses from those centuries that stand on the one long main street.

The parish church is reached by narrow lanes between eighteenth-century cottages which end in a secluded enclave. As the approach is from the west one sees first the handsome west tower, built of the

Opposite: The church is in a quiet corner of the town off the main street. The tower, a late addition of 1549, is constructed of local red sandstone with buff limestone decoration. The latter gives it something of the character of the towers of adjacent Somerset.

Right: The magnificent south aisle was built in 1526 by John Lane, a wealthy cloth merchant. He is buried inside and an inscription commemorating him and his family runs along the window sills. The chapel has the huge windows typical of late Perpendicular Gothic.

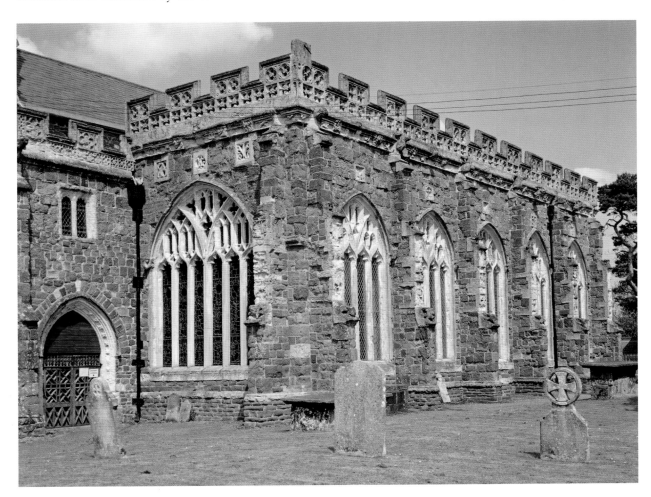

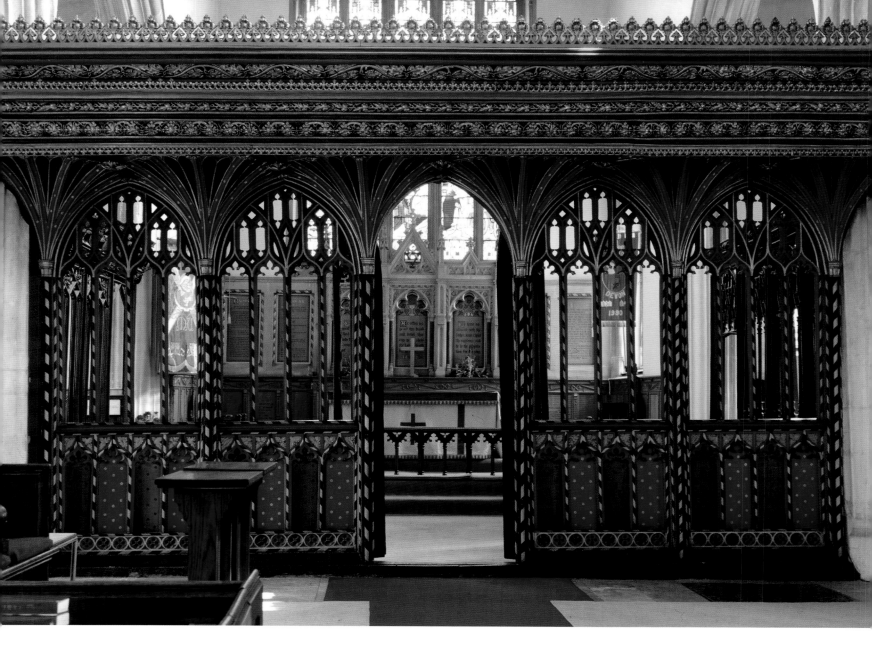

red sandstone that underlies much of the county. The windows and decorative features are picked out in silvery grey limestone. Above the west window there is a large panel showing the Crucifixion, with smaller panels showing the Virgin and St John on either side. Above these there is a clock set under a gable of the same limestone. The presence of the 1540s arms of the then bishop of Exeter shows the tower is of that date. The builders of the tower were clearly familiar with the towers of neighbouring Somerset built during the previous century, but the decoration does not quite reach the same standard. The storm clouds of the Reformation were already over England when this tower was being built.

The church behind the tower is dated a little earlier but is built in the same uniformly Perpendicular Gothic style. A walk around the outside shows that the building is very broad for its length and that this is due to the

existence of not one but two aisles on the south side of the nave. The outer is a mortuary chapel for the Lane family, which was added to the church in 1526. John Lane was a wealthy cloth merchant who died shortly after the chapel was added. The chapel, or aisle, is the most spectacular part of the exterior. The walls are more glass than stone, in the Perpendicular fashion. The buttresses are decorated with carvings of symbols of Lane's trade, such as cloth, shears and the ships used to carry his goods abroad. A pretty pierced parapet runs along the top together with a weather-worn frieze showing scenes from the life of Christ. Below the windows there is another frieze with an inscription placed so that all can read it:

In honour of God and his blessed mother Mary Remeb the souls of John Lane w a pat nst & ave meri [i.e. with a pater noster and ave Maria] and the sawle of Thomsyn

The fifteenth-century rood screen runs the full width of the church. The base is a solid dado and above that there is open tracery work. This supports a coved section leading to the intricately carved rood loft. Originally this would have held the figures of the crucified Christ, the Virgin Mary and St John.

his wiffe to have in memory with all other their children & friends of youre owne chyryty which were founders of this Chapell & here lieth in Sepulther The yere of ower Lorde God a thousand five hundrith syx and twenty God of his grace on ther boyth sowles to have mercy and finally bring them to the eternal glory. Amen for Chryty.

This mixture of piety and the desire to be remembered for posterity is typical of the wealthy of the late Middle Ages.

The pleasure and interest one feels on visiting this church increase inside. The interior has a sense of spaciousness, due as in so many Perpendicular churches to the wide arcade arches supported by slim piers. The

A rood screen detail. The paint has been renewed according to the original scheme.

abundance of brilliant colours from floor to ceiling strikes at once and the plush red carpets give a sense of luxury. The rood screen is outstanding in a county famous for its screens. It stretches across the entire width of the church, taking in the chapels on either side of the chancel as well as the chancel itself. It is ablaze with red, green and much gilt. The lower stage is a solid dado, and then comes an open 'window' stage of thin mullions with tracery in the arches. Above this a ribbed coving reaches upwards and forwards to support a high parapet decorated with the most intricate carving in four bands. The rood itself, a crucifix with figures of the Virgin and St John that would have stood above the centre of the parapet, was of course removed during the Reformation. The paint is quite recent, doubtless the latest of many repaintings undertaken over the last 500 years as a matter of necessity. Modern conservation work attempts to detect and reproduce original colour schemes of art like this. The short screen that separates the chancel from a chapel to its north is in sharp contrast to the rood screen. Here the unpainted oak is now almost black with age. The upper part is composed mainly of heraldic shields, and the little decoration avoids the pointed arches of Gothic as if the carver had a feeling for the coming Renaissance art forms.

From floor to screens to roof, the colour continues. The wagon roof runs the entire length of the building without any division between chancel and nave (see page 88). This type of roof, which is a speciality of Devon, gets its name from old-fashioned canvas-covered wagons – as seen in so many western films. Such roofs can be quite plain structures panelled only with longitudinal and transverse ribs with limewashed in-filling. At Cullompton all the panels have decorative edging and diagonal cross-ribs. All the junctions have bosses that, like the ribs, are picked out in gilt, all against a blue background.

John Lane's wealth is even more evident inside his chapel than outside. It has a fan-vaulted stone roof, one of the most spectacular of all Perpendicular architectural creations. Since the chapel is lower than the nave its presence is the more overpowering. The reason for the name is evident. In each bay of the chapel ribbed structures resembling hand fans spring from each of the four corners and touch near the centre. Colour plays no part here. The fascination is the web of thin stone lines curving in all directions. Lane may have got his inspiration from a similar chapel at nearby Ottery St Mary built only a few years

The stone fan vault in the Lane chapel. Such roofs are justifiably regarded as the supreme achievement of medieval masons. Each bay of the roof has four inverted ribbed cones springing from the corners and meeting in the centre, resembling four fans.

Opposite: Wagon roofs are characteristic of West Country churches but few are decorated as sumptuously as this. Each panel has cross-ribs and bosses at the intersections.

earlier. Neither church is very far from Sherbourne Abbey in Dorset, where the first large-scale fan vault was raised in the 1450s. Lane's tomb, and that of his wife, is marked by a simple stone in the floor, its brass effigy now lost. Perhaps the lack of a flamboyant monument so common in the medieval and post-medieval periods indicates that Lane was a man of modest pride in his achievements rather than one of overweening vanity. In most churches it is generally a very human mixture of wealth, pride and piety that has left us such treasuries of beautiful architecture and art.

10

ST MARY AND ALL SAINTS, FOTHERINGHAY, NORTHAMPTONSHIRE

A Noble Church Built for Noble Patrons

FOTHERINGHAY IS A SMALL, QUIET village away from main roads in gently undulating countryside on the banks of the River Nene about six miles north of the town of Oundle. Most of the houses and cottages are built of the local creamy limestone and stand in harmonious visual unity. Although today Fotheringhay may be small and peaceful, that was not always the case. The name

Opposite: The River Nene runs in front of the south side of the church built in 1390–1440 by the first three Dukes of York. Its oddly truncated appearance is due to the demolition of the chancel during the Reformation.

Right: The west tower is unusual in starting square and becoming octagonal in the upper stage. The large Perpendicular windows flood the interior with light.

Opposite: The short, broad interior from the west end. The atmosphere is one of airiness and colour. Heraldic shields fill the spandrels of the arcade arches.

is well known to historians studying the fifteenth and sixteenth centuries when it was the scene of tumultuous events.

In the mid-fourteenth century the lands and church of Fotheringhay came into the possession of the crown during the reign of Edward III who gave them to his fifth son, Edmund of Langley (1341–1402). Since that time few churches outside London or Windsor have had more extensive royal connections than Fotheringhay. Edmund was created first Duke of York by his elder brother Richard II in 1375, thus founding the Yorkist branch of the Plantagenet dynasty. If Tewkesbury (see chapter 3) saw the bloody fighting that ended the main chapter of the Wars of the Roses between the Yorkist descendants of Edmund Langley

and the Lancastrian descendants of his brother John of Gaunt then the seeds of those wars may be said to have been sown at Fotheringhay. Edmund rebuilt the existing twelfth-century Norman castle and church on a grand scale just a few hundred yards apart. The best overall view of the church is from the south on the opposite bank of the River Nene. From here its impressive height and curiously truncated length are seen without distraction from the neighbouring houses hidden behind. The new church was to be part of a collegiate foundation that was also to serve the parish. There was an exceptionally long chancel for the members of the college, which was to consist of a master, 12 fellows, eight clerks and 13 choristers. The shorter, but still impressive, nave was for the people of the parish. Edmund died before the church was completed, and this and the other college buildings were completed by the second and third dukes. The latter were buried in the collegiate chancel. Richard III, descendent of Edmund and last of the Plantagenet kings, was born at the castle in 1452. In the 1530s Henry VIII regarded collegiate communities as equivalent to monasteries so the college was dissolved and the property later sold to the Duke of Northumberland. He demolished the chancel of the church and the domestic buildings but the nave had to be retained as it had parochial status.

These events explain the church we see today. What appears as a disproportionately short church was formerly over twice the length before demolition of the chancel. However, what remains is still a noble building, tall with two storeys of large windows in the aisles and clerestory. These are characteristic of Gothic Perpendicular architecture and have been described as 'more glass than wall'. The tall tower starts square before becoming octagonal in the upper stages. This is unusual but not unique as there are other examples in Northamptonshire. It makes for an interesting vertical element on an exterior that has a quiet, unfussy dignity.

Some churches impress without but disappoint within or vice versa. Not so here. The interior is wonderfully bright, airy, spacious and colourful. Brightness comes from the two tiers of clear glass windows. The airiness and spaciousness come from the wide arches of the arcade, separating nave and aisles,

The mid-fifteenth-century pulpit has been recently repainted to the original colour scheme. The original small medieval tester (sounding board) is beneath the larger eighteenth-century addition.

which are supported by slender pillars that seem to allow space to float around them in a way characteristic of East Anglian churches (see chapter 8). Because the nave is relatively short the altar, now set against the blocked-up arch into the former chancel, and the clergy who officiate there are in close contact with the congregation, as modern church people prefer. In early Gothic churches altars were at the far end of chancels, stretching into the distance with a rood screen further reducing contact between priest and people.

There are various splashes of bright colour throughout the church. Just below the windows lines of heraldic shields are reminders of the aristocratic families connected with the church. The twentieth century has draped a large union jack across a pier at the back. The rare medieval stone pulpit is prominently placed to provide a pattern of many colours. It was donated by the first Yorkist king, Edward IV, brother of Richard III. It was repainted and gilded in 1968 using traces of original colouring as a guide. Its large tester, or sounding board, is eighteenth century, but within this there is a pretty little stone-ribbed medieval tester. The pulpit is a precious survival because most medieval pulpits were wooden and have disappeared.

The second and third Dukes of York, who were involved in building the college, were buried in the chancel. When this was demolished in 1556 the monuments then exposed to the weather fell into disrepair. When Elizabeth I visited the church in 1573 she was distressed to see them in that state and ordered new monuments to be erected in the nave. The two are now prominent features on either side of the altar. They are architectural structures without effigies. The details are now entirely classical Renaissance and show clearly the gap of a century between them and the deaths of the people they commemorate.

The handsome set of eighteenth-century box pews is a welcome addition to the interior. The light brown wood blends well with the cream-coloured limestone walls and they are not obtrusively high as they are in many places, nor are there too many of them. The broad central aisle that separates them is wide enough for 12 people to walk abreast and enhances the feeling of spaciousness of the interior.

There is one exception to the clear glass in the church. In 1975 the Richard III society commissioned a stained glass window that shows the arms of the first three Dukes of York and Richard III in richly glowing colours.

Fotheringhay has a later, grimmer place in English history. When Mary, Queen of Scots, was expelled from Scotland in

Above: The Royal Arms of George III (reigned 1760–1820). Arms of the reigning monarchs as Supreme Governors of the Church of England were first ordered to be placed in churches by Henry VIII but became largely obsolete during the reign of Queen Victoria.

Right: The tomb of Richard, third Duke of York (died 1460), erected by Elizabeth I in 1573 was a replacement of the original that at the time had become derelict outside in the ruined chancel. It is purely architectural, without an effigy.

1578 she fled to England hoping for protection from her cousin Elizabeth I. She was regarded as a threat to Elizabeth's throne and was kept in close confinement in various castles and stately homes, ending up in Fotheringhay Castle in 1585. By that time there was a growing suspicion that she was involved in the plot against Elizabeth. On 14 October 1586 a state trial was held in the great hall of the castle. It was by all accounts a travesty of justice. Mary was found guilty of high treason, and, after a period of agonising, Elizabeth signed the death warrant. On 8 February 1587 Mary was beheaded in the same great hall before a large crowd. In July of that year her body was taken to Peterborough Cathedral, ten miles away, and buried at dead of night. In 1612 her body was transferred to Westminster Abbey by order of her son James I of England and VI of Scotland, where it now lies alongside Elizabeth. Very little remains of the castle, only the earthen motte and a single fragment of masonry.

Being a Catholic and rejecting the doctrines and services of the reformed religion, Mary had presumably little to do with the church close to the castle during the 60 months she stayed there. However, in our own times of reconciliation between Christians, in 1987, the four-hundredth anniversary of Mary's death, on a Sunday in February closest to her death, a Catholic priest celebrated a requiem mass for Mary in the presence of a large congregation of Catholics and Anglicans. So are kept alive the memories of a long line of royal connections with this wonderful church.

A stained glass window inserted by the Richard III Society in 1975. The king's arms are centre, top. He was born in Fotheringhay Castle on 2 October 1452 and killed at the Battle of Bosworth Field in 1485. Other arms include those of the first three Dukes of York who built the church.

All that remains of Fotheringhay Castle is the earthen motte and a lump of masonry. Mary Queen of Scots was executed in the Great Hall in 1587. The church is a few hundred yards to the left.

11
ST NONNA, ALTARNUN, CORNWALL

A Quintessential Cornish Church

Cornwall and its churches have a character distinct from that of the rest of England. This is partly because of the varied landscapes. Two coastlines, to the north and south, have hundreds of miles of cliffs, small coves, long sandy beaches and scores of small fishing villages. The farming country above the cliffs can be swept by wind and rain or bathed in warm sunshine depending on the season. Further inland shelter can be found in steep-sided combes. There are several expanses of moorland. Visitors enter the county across Bodmin Moor, one of the few remaining untamed areas of England, bleak

Below: The simple window tracery also reflects the difficulty of carving in granite.

Opposite: Even at a distance the relatively austere appearance of the fifteenth-century church tells of the hardness of the local granite used in its building, which made it difficult to provide decorative details. The tall tower and low body of the church are characteristically Cornish.

The south aisle looking into the nave. The slender granite piers are monoliths from nearby Bodmin Moor. Wagon roofs and naves without upper clerestory windows are common throughout Cornwall.

The considerable width of the church is emphasised by the seventeenth-century altar rails running from wall to wall without break.

The balusters of the altar rails spell out in one letter each the names of the rector and churchwardens who installed them. These refer to (Samson) Cowl, a churchwarden.

of St Piran, half buried in the sands near Penhale for centuries, is one of the earliest in England.

Buildings and building materials do much to define the character of the region and this is especially true of Cornwall. It is axiomatic that what is seen above ground in this context is related to what is below ground, i.e. to the geology. Cornwall, Devon and Cumbria are the only English counties where granite is quarried. As a result it is seen everywhere – in cottages, farmhouses, public buildings, harbour walls, quays and, of course, churches. When seen in weathered exteriors it appears as a uniform silver-grey but it consists of several minerals, which can be seen in polished gravestones or interiors. There is silica in the form of quartz and several complex silicate compounds formed geologically when silica fused with metal oxides such as sodium, aluminium and iron. All of these minerals are among the physically hardest and chemically most inert of any natural compound, and as a result granite is the most durable of all the English building stones. This is fortuitous in a county that can experience hard weather. The rain always seems a little wetter in Cornwall and the winds from the Atlantic coast a little stronger, carrying with them salt-laden air. Many of the limestones and sandstones widely used elsewhere would have a short life here. The hardness of granite has its disadvantages. Excavating at the quarries and the subsequent cutting into building-size pieces were arduous jobs, and until the nineteenth century they were done with hand-worked saws. Church masons found it impossible to create the finely and intricately carved window tracery, parapets, finials and buttresses seen in earlier chapters. As a result Cornish church exteriors are plainer, more masculine one might say, than their counterparts in the Cotswolds or East Anglia. Cornwall's second most important building stone is slate, another hard silicate that is impervious to water and has the rare ability to be cleaved into thin sheets. Cornish slate has been exported all over England for use as roof tiles. In addition large slate flagstones make handsome floors in most Cornish churches, adding to the rugged character. So, from roofs to walls and floors, granite and slate are the building blocks, literally, of Cornish churches. Though these are not showy stones they are admirably suited to their environment.

The village of Altarnun is on the northern edge of Bodmin Moor, only a little distance from the main road that runs down the spine of Cornwall taking heavy tourist traffic to the county's resorts. The distance is enough, however, to give residents and visitors peace

and forbidding yet attracting visitors because of those very things. Cornish churches can be found in all these settings. Morwenstow church on the north coast is only a few yards from the cliff's edge; many shipwrecked sailors are buried in its churchyard. Gunwalloe church, surrounded by sand dunes on the south coast, is only a few yards above the high tide mark. There are several moorland churches, including the subject of this chapter. Every fishing village has its parish church, many close to the quaysides.

The character of these churches is also a result of Cornwall's history and culture. The Anglo-Saxons only managed to penetrate into Cornwall in the ninth century so the people preserved their Celtic identity longer and more securely than the rest of England. They still do so today. Many towns and villages are named after the Celtic saints from Wales, Ireland and Brittany who evangelised the area between the fifth and eighth centuries: St Ives, St Enodoc, St Buryan and St Neot, to name only a few. Their lives are shrouded in fanciful legends but they were real people with real achievements. The tiny chapel while providing easy access to the market towns of Launceston to the north and Bodmin to the south. The names of some Cornish villages disguise their association with a saint. Altarnun is 'the altar of Saint Nonna', i.e. the place of the church dedicated to Saint Nonna. She was the mother of Saint David, who left her native Wales to come here in 527. The village has a single main street lined with granite cottages of exposed or limewashed stone. The church – granite too, of course – lies at the western end of the street and is built into the side of a hill as though for protection from the gales blowing across the moor. A small river crossed by a stone bridge separates the churchyard from the street. At 109 feet the west tower is one of the tallest in Cornwall, some three times higher than the main body of the church, which, like most Cornish village churches, lacks height due to the absence of a second storey of windows in the nave above the aisles. The building appears to be uniformly fifteenth-century Perpendicular throughout but there are traces of its Norman origins. It is a curious fact that the numerous churches built in Cornwall by the invading Normans in the twelfth century were left untouched for hundreds of years until a veritable spree of rebuilding took place in the later Middle Ages. Invariably, however, some notable Norman features were left intact and serve as markers for future generations.

Once inside, the plainness of the window tracery and other decorative features is immediately apparent. The interior consists of a nave, with north and south aisles, that has no structural division from the chancel. The arcades separating the nave from the aisles have widely spaced slim piers allowing clear views across the width of the building, making it appear even broader than it is. The piers are carved from 'moorstones', monolithic pieces of granite found on the surface of the moor. As already mentioned the nave has no clerestory windows and the lack of height is felt at once. However, the clear glass aisle windows provide adequate light. The nave and aisles have the wagon roofs characteristic of the West Country (see chapter 9). A separated chancel area is provided by a rood screen which runs the full width of the church from north to south wall. At the centre there is a pair of heavy doors, solid below with open tracery in the upper parts. Within the chancel the altar is further separated by a seventeenth-century communion rail, again running across the whole building. Its turned balusters with square bases and tops and a top rail have Classical details. The square tops of the balusters each have a carved letter, so that walking

the full length of the 115 balusters one reads: 'John Ruddle, minister of Launceston prebendary of Exon and Vicar of this parish anno 1684. William Prideaux and Samson Cowl churchwardens'. (Exon refers to the diocese of Exeter of which Cornwall was then a part.)

The church has a set of 79 original benches, one of the largest collections of their kind in England. They are notable for their carved end pieces of unusual and interesting variety. Only a few have sacred iconography, such as the Five Wounds of Christ, angels and symbols of the saints. The most interesting show village people in various occupations. There are also fantastic creatures such as green men and mermen. A large number show fruit and foliage of various kinds. The carver of all these has made himself known on one of the ends where the inscription beneath an angel reads: 'Robert Daye

The heavy oak doors in the rood screen leading into the chancel from the nave.

Maker Of This Work 1510 – 1530'. A guidebook to the entire collection can be purchased in the church.

The font is the only survival from the Norman church referred to previously. 'A magnificent piece', it is unusually large with a square bowl on a cylindrical stem. The corners of the bowl have bearded men and large rosettes on the sides. Traces of original colour are visible. It is perhaps significant that throughout England, not only in Cornwall, hundreds of Norman fonts have survived in churches that were completely rebuilt in later periods. Apart from the saving of the expense of carving new fonts, perhaps they were retained because people of the time were reluctant to throw away the font where their parents and many generations previously were baptised. These fonts represented a very personal link to their families' histories at a time when few people ever left their place of birth.

A rural church may have its rural problems. At the time of my visit, a notice near the door read, 'We apologise if you find some parts of the church dirty and seemingly neglected. The church is plagued with a colony of bats with obvious consequences!' No apology is needed. The church is neither dirty nor neglected.

Altarnun church like many others in Cornwall has relatively little of the highest aesthetic quality but much that is lovable and much that is moving, and the distinct appearance of these churches is often made profound by their diverse and moving locations.

Above: Three of the interesting set of early-sixteenth-century carved bench ends. Left to right: Symbols of St Peter (keys) and St Paul (sword), the patrons of the diocese of Exeter; a jester; a viol player.

Left: The twelfth-century Norman font survives from the earlier church. Traces of original colour remain on the rosettes and corner faces.

12

ST LEONARD, MIDDLETON, GREATER MANCHESTER

A Late-Medieval Church Overlooking a Pennine Landscape of Hills, Mills and Factories

I N SAXON TIMES, MIDDLETON was a village, which later grew to a township, seven miles north-east of Manchester. Since the early twentieth century, progressive expansion of the city has joined the two together so that those driving through it today on the main road between Manchester and Rochdale might get the misleading impression that Middleton is like any characterless outer suburb of a northern city. To its north, west and east the built landscape gives way to fields, but what distinguishes Middleton from an ordinary suburb is that it lies in the western foothills of the Pennines. The centre of the town is on lower

The external features of the church, which presides high over the town, are from *c*.1524. They are all made from Pennine sandstone except for the wooden top storey of the tower, which was added in 1667.

A view eastwards from the churchyard with the Pennine hills in the distance. When seen in bright sunlight the nineteenth-century mills and their chimneys did not seem as 'dark' and 'satanic' as William Blake described them in the hymn-poem 'Jerusalem'.

ground and the streets radiating from it climb quite steeply. From many street corners and in between houses there are distant views to the Pennines. There are a small number of medieval buildings, including St Leonard's, but the main impression is of the mid- and late nineteenth century, with row upon row of terraced houses built of the local millstone grit sandstone or brick. They are of the two-up two-down type, many of them letting directly on to the streets in a way made familiar to the nation from television's *Coronation Street*, set in neighbouring Salford. On the growing edges of the town there are, of course, many more modern houses. In the nineteenth century the cotton industry came to much of the area, Middleton included, creating vast mills with tall chimneys. The cotton has gone now and the mills have been converted to engineering works, showrooms, cash-and-carry stores and the like.

The parish church of St Leonard is boldly and prominently sited on top of a steep hill about 200 yards north of the town centre. From the spacious hilltop churchyard, crammed with blackened sandstone monuments both grandiose and humble, there are views over the town for about six miles to Manchester in the south and Oldham and the Pennines in the east. The mills and their chimneys were once visible in the foreground and in the middle distance

The Norman arch into the west tower shows the earlier origin of the church. Its original round arch was reset to a Gothic point at some later time.

The late-seventeenth-century 'horse box' pew of the local Hopwood family gave them complete privacy.

creating a scene that the Salford painter L. S. Lowry (1887–1976) would have appreciated and that would have rung a chord with William Blake, author of the well-known mystical poem-hymn 'Jerusalem'.

The church is built of coarse-grained Pennine sandstone. Like the gravestones its gritty surface has caught the smoke of thousands of domestic and industrial chimneys over the last 200 years, but a considerable flaking away of the stone has revealed an attractive golden colour beneath in many places. The church consists of an aisled nave, chancel and west tower. The tower has a distinctive, weather-boarded top stage with four gables. Externally the church appears to be completely Perpendicular Gothic and we know that a Middleton man, Cardinal Thomas Langley (c.1370–1427), bishop of Durham, Keeper of the Privy Seal and Chancellor to Henry IV, paid for a substantially new building in 1412 that he himself consecrated. In the following century the local lord of the manor, Richard Assheton, remodelled the church again in 1524, leaving only the tower and sumptuous south porch of Langley's church.

However, when we enter the church we can immediately see its much earlier origins. The arch from the nave into the west tower is Norman with the chevron (zig-zag) decoration that was ubiquitous throughout much of the twelfth century. In a later

The lower part of the c.1530 rood screen shows something of the coming Renaissance in England.

resetting the originally round arch was made pointed in the Gothic manner. The rest of the interior is mainly the result of Assheton's rebuilding.

The most interesting feature from the late Middle Ages is a chancel window of c.1530 commemorating the battle of Flodden in 1513, in which Henry VIII's forces defeated those of James IV of Scotland in the north of England. Richard Assheton took 16 Middleton archers and a chaplain to the battle. The window shows the Assheton family in the upper half, and below, chaplain Henricus Tayler in front of the archers. They, like the family above, are all shown kneeling. The archers all carry their longbows with their individual names inscribed below the figures. This must be one of the earliest 'war memorial' windows in England. Richard Assheton was knighted for his services to the king, and his rebuilding of the parish church may have been connected with the victory and his knighthood.

The rood screen has its original dado (lower solid part). This also is of the time of Sir Richard or a little later and, with its square panels of heraldic arms, it is an early indicator of the coming Renaissance in England, when Classical forms replaced Gothic. There are several early sixteenth-century Assheton brasses in the chancel floor, including one for an Assheton rector. In the south aisle is the large family pew of the Hopwood family from nearby Hopwood Hall. Late seventeenth-century structures such as this are aptly called 'horse box' pews, solid below with twisted balusters above. Remarkably, there is another interesting window showing Middleton men who fought in a war nearly 400 years after Flodden. Glass from 1903 by G. F. Bodley, a leading architect and artist of the time, shows Boer War soldiers with their equipment and a pack horse. Its commissioning may have been inspired by the Flodden window. Of a slightly later date is some gem-like glass of Christopher Whall, a follower of the Pre-Raphaelites (see chapter 25).

Visitors to Middleton parish church come away with an unusual mixture of impressions in which images of the mid- and late Middle Ages mingle with those of a recent but rapidly disappearing northern industrial past.

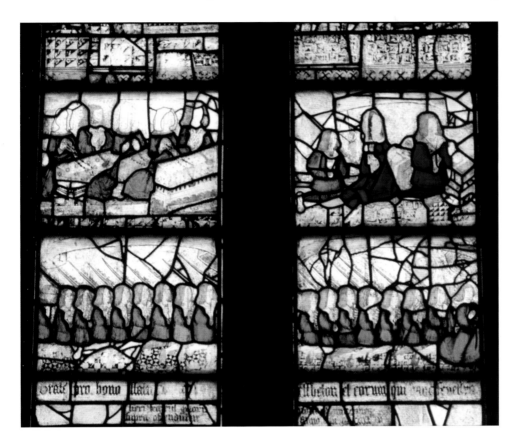

Above: With glass from 1530 this is one of the earliest war memorial windows in England. It commemorates the Battle of Flodden in 1513, to which Richard Assheton, the lord of the manor, sent 16 Middleton archers and a chaplain (lower panels). The archers in blue carry their longbows, which are just visible. The chaplain, Henricus Taylor, kneels in front (right). The Assheton family are in the top panels.

Left: The involvement of Middleton men in another war nearly 400 years after Flodden shows them in uniform with a pack horse during the Boer War of 1899–1901.

13

ST PETER AND ST PAUL, EXTON, LEICESTERSHIRE

Five Centuries of Family Monuments in a Rural Westminster Abbey

THE VILLAGE OF EXTON IS a few miles northeast of the small market town of Oakham; both are close to Rutland Water. It is a place that few will find by chance as it is separated from the nearest main road by several miles of country lanes. It is in what was the county of Rutland, the smallest in England before it was absorbed into Leicestershire for administrative purposes in 1974. The old county name survives for many everyday purposes as does its entirely rural character, which gives a glimpse of England before the Industrial Revolution.

Monument to John Harrington (died 1524) and his wife. Finely carved in English alabaster, the emphasis is on Christian piety and prayer.

The fourteenth-century church now stands alone in the park of Exton Hall (just visible left background). Monuments to its occupants over more than 500 years fill the church. The village surrounded the church until it was banished to outside the park in the eighteenth century.

The village consists of pretty cottages around a green encircled by trees. It has the most traditional and attractive of layouts that is, however, one not common today. It appears to be a village without a parish church, but a high stone wall stretching well beyond the cottages tells of parkland surrounding a stately home. In the Middle Ages the manor was the basis of rural feudal society, which consisted of the house of the lord of the manor, a village and a church all grouped closely together in feudal interdependency. In the eighteenth century the landowning aristocracy looked for privacy, not community, and villages were often banished to a place outside the park where that interdependency still existed between landlord and tenants, employer and labourers but at a greater distance. For legal as well as practical reasons the parish church was not so easily

The monument to Robert Kelway (died 1580), a wealthy lawyer, rises from floor to rafters and is typical of the grandest Elizabethan type. The recumbent effigy is within an architectural surround of multi-coloured marbles now in the classical Renaissance style. All the work is of the highest quality.

Monument to Robert Kelway (detail). He is surrounded by his family, here his daughter and granddaughter. The exquisite modelling of their features and clothing is apparent.

The church dates from the late thirteenth to the mid-fourteenth century. The east midland counties are part of the limestone belt that runs across England from south-west to north-east. Here the stone is known misleadingly as ironstone because of the high concentration of iron oxides that stain it light brown. It is of this stone that the church is built. The church has a tall west steeple characteristic of so many in this part of England. It is from these that the term 'steeple chasing' in modern horseracing derives. In the eighteenth century the local gentry, farmers and young bloods would race each other across country using the village church steeples as markers. In this flat countryside it is possible to see up to half a dozen steeples from the same spot. The Exton steeple has an unusual three-stage design. There is a square tower below with bell openings, battlements and corner turret pinnacles. Above is an octagonal stage and above that a short spire. The body of the church consists of chancel, nave with aisles and two transepts.

The setting alone would justify a visit to Exton church but that is only an introduction. 'There are no churches in Rutland and few in England in which English funerary sculpture from the sixteenth to the eighteenth century can be studied so profitably and enjoyably as Exton.' The families living at Old Hall and then New Hall were similar to others throughout the country in that they wished to be buried and remembered not in some distant cathedral, abbey church or even a local town church but in their own parish church close to their ancestral home. The result over the centuries was buildings that are part parish church, part family mausoleum, where every area — chancel, transepts, nave and aisles — came to be filled with monuments of a size and quality that only those with wealth and taste could commission. As well as providing examples of the work of leading sculptors of the day, they give interesting insights into changing social and religious attitudes.

The monuments that are illustrated are described in chronological order. The oldest shown, but not the oldest in the church, is for John Harrington (died 1524) and his wife. It is the standard medieval type where the deceased lie on a tomb chest with hands joined piously in prayer. Between the twelfth and sixteenth centuries bishops, abbots and priests were shown in this way, lying alone. Laymen usually lie alongside their wives. In this monument a tiny angel supports the pillow on which the lady's head rests. At her feet two pet dogs (symbols of fidelity) nibble at the hems of her skirt. The whole monument

removed though it was not impossible. Therefore, for the last 200 years some parish churches have been hidden within parks while the villages are without. The villagers and visitors have always retained the right of access to these parish churches and their churchyards.

Exton Park as it is now called contained the original Tudor house of a series of families who succeeded each other over several centuries. The parish church was only a few hundred yards away surrounded by cottages before the latter were expelled. The house burnt down in 1810, but the ruins were preserved as a picturesque feature when a lavish replacement was built a little further from the church immediately afterwards. Thus we have a grouping of Old Hall, New Hall and church, each visible from the other within the seclusion of rolling wooded parkland.

is carved from alabaster, which was the preferred material for the finest quality work. It is a crystalline form of calcium sulphate mined in Derbyshire and Nottinghamshire, which is hard enough to take a polish that gives it a translucent waxy appearance not inappropriate for the depiction of the dead.

The monument for Robert Kelway who died in 1581 occupies the whole of the south transept. He was a lawyer whose son married a Harrington heiress. The monument is at once similar to and different from the Harrington monument. The deceased lies in death on a tomb chest, hands piously joined. His son and daughter-in-law kneel either side on a step below the chest. Their hands too are joined in prayer. Behind them are the small figures of Kelway's grandchildren. All of this continues a tradition of Christian piety in church monuments but here the resemblance to the earlier tomb ends. This is now a breath-taking exercise in flamboyance. In the Elizabethan period, the chest and effigy type of monuments of the Middle Ages were given an 'architectural' surround made up of columns supporting a superstructure, all rendered in the new classical forms of the Italian Renaissance then becoming known in England. The details were as yet imperfectly known, and they were mixed with other non-classical forms in an undisciplined way. The use of resplendently coloured imported marbles, bright paints and gilt reflects the exuberance and self-confidence of the age. There is so much to see that they are always a joy to examine and the colour brings a cheerful bling to interiors that are often rather sombre. Kelway lies within a semicircular recess with a coffered vault that is itself part of a large assembly of four Corinthian columns and an architrave. This rises to yet greater heights with another structure containing heraldry flanked by two large obelisks. Unlike many of this type, which were designed to impress more by size than artistic quality, the Kelway monument is equally impressive at close-up. The details of the carving are superb in the portraiture, the clothing, the garlands and other decorative work.

In the chancel there is a slightly later Elizabethan monument for Sir James Harrington, who died in 1591, and his wife. It represents a newly devised type popular in 1580–1630. The two near life-size figures face each other across a prayer desk. There is again much use of coloured stones in a large architectural surround.

The monument in the north aisle for Anne, Lady Bruce of Kinross, daughter of the first Lord Harrington, takes us to 1627. 'It is a work of great importance and

exceptional beauty.' The monument is within a few feet of that of John Harrington and his wife (above). At first sight the two are not dissimilar, as the deceased in both lie on simple tomb chests. However, the 100 years between them, during which the Middle Ages faded and the Renaissance began, represent a sea change in the attitude to the representation of the human body. The Harrington figures lie stiffly, with no attempt to show them as real people. Their bodies are concealed under rigid draperies, and their facial expressions show nothing of personality. The key feature is the hands joined in prayer, a reminder to the viewer of the pre-eminent importance of Christian faith and the relative unimportance of the physical body. In contrast,

Monument to Sir James Harrington (died 1591) and his wife. Two kneeling figures facing each other across a prayer desk surrounded by architecture is typical of the late Elizabethan and Jacobean periods.

Lady Bruce is modelled in white marble on a black and white chest. The most important contrast is the way in which real human anatomy and personality are portrayed. The face shows the serenity of a woman dying rather than inertly dead. Although the body is concealed beneath a sheet, its life-like contours are clearly visible and even the folds of the sheet are realistically carved. Renaissance art, especially when compared with medieval art, emphasised the beauty and nobility of the human body as the creation of God and the importance of individual personality. It is rare to be able to see the contrast between two philosophies so close together.

In the seventeenth century the Harringtons sold the estate to the Hicks family, Viscounts Camden. Sir Baptist Hicks, the first Viscount, is commemorated in magnificent style in Chipping Camden church, Gloucestershire. The third Viscount, who died in 1683, was clearly intent on doing the same at Exton. His wall monument fills one side of the north transept. It is among the first that established a style that became standard for the wealthiest and most powerful in the land throughout the eighteenth century. The deceased were no longer reposed in death or kneeling in prayer but standing up and very much alive. Neither was there any hint of religious feeling; that was replaced by swaggering self-assurance. For the next 100 years the aristocracy commemorated in church monuments would stare down at the viewer in poses that showed that they were the owners and rulers of land. No expense was spared in employing the finest sculptors of the day. This particular work, which rises from floor to ceiling height, is by Grinling Gibbons and the accounts show that he was paid £1,000. (In comparison, one of the labourers on the estate might have earned £3 in a year at the time.) Gibbons, of course, was more famous as a woodcarver who created vividly realistic carvings of garlands, flowers, musical instruments, angels and the like, in great country houses, cathedrals and public buildings. He was clearly as competent working in stone. The Viscount is dressed in Roman costume, a monumental convention at a time when England aspired to emulate the imperial power of a former empire. He stands on the opposite side of an urn to his fourth wife. His former deceased wives and

This monument to Lady Harrington (died 1627) in white marble is an instructive contrast to that of John Harrington crafted 100 years earlier (see page 107). This Renaissance work now celebrates the human body as something important in its own right, with real-life features, body outline and drapery, in contrast to the stiff formality of the medieval effigies.

his 19 children by them are shown in medallions on either side. Two tall obelisks, left and right, rest on black spheres and support two vases. The architectural part is completed by an open pediment. Art aside, the dynastic self-regard inherent in this type of display will amaze the twenty-first-century viewer, but that of course is part of its fascination today.

The eighteenth-century monuments are, by comparison, relatively restrained. By this time the Hicks family had sold out to the Noel family, Earls of Gainsborough. Their best monument is that of Elizabeth, Countess of the 4th Earl of Gainsborough, who died in 1771. Joseph Nollekens, again one of the most fashionable sculptors of the late eighteenth

The monument by Grinling Gibbons to Baptist Hicks, 3rd Viscount Camden (died 1683), heralds in a new spirit in funerary works. He and his fourth wife, both in Roman dress, stand upright in supremely self-confident poses, lords of all they survey, no trace of piety. His previous wives and 19 children are shown in medallions. The massive surround has characteristically Baroque opulence and drama.

century, was commissioned. The countess is shown seated on a striated sarcophagus with a mourning cherub above. She points to medallions of her first and second husbands while a cherub flutters on top. This represents a newer, gentler approach, with the first hint of the sentimentality of the nineteenth century. This century saw the rapid decline and eventual passing of the great period of English church monuments. In the twentieth century there was neither the money nor the inclination to continue. Even the most aristocratic are now content with small, soberly worded wall tablets (see Introduction).

The presence of the families at the two Halls is further emphasised by their funeral banners and armour which hang high up on the walls on either side of the nave. Sadly decaying, they are a symbolic reminder of past glories.

The quality of many of the monuments at Exton is worthy of Westminster Abbey or some great metropolitan museum. It is remarkable, but not unusual, to find them instead in such a remote and rustic setting, free of jostling, noisy crowds. However, this shows that the aristocracy had their hearts in their country homes and wished to be remembered there. You can spend several hours in this church without seeing another soul, and since there is hardly a sound from the park outside your only companions are the echoes of your own footsteps as you wander amongst the monuments. It is not necessary to be psychic or sentimental to feel the ghostly presences that lurk within the figures frozen in stone. The visitor to Exton enjoys a uniquely English combination of diverse things: history and fine art in an old church adjacent to the two stately homes, within a picturesque park with a handsome village at its gates – all tucked away in a hidden countryside.

The monument to the Countess of Gainsborough (died 1771) introduces a gentler, more sentimental, spirit as she lies dying on a sarcophagus pointing to angels and family medallions above.

The nave is hung with ornamental banners and armour used at family funerals in the sixteenth and seventeenth centuries.

CHURCHES OF THE SEVENTEENTH AND EIGHTEENTH CENTURIES

New Ideas from Italy but Old Traditions Persist

The enthusiasm for church building continued in England right up to the end of the Middle Ages and into the early Tudor period. Some of the finest parish churches were built in the fifteenth century, including the great 'Wool Churches' of East Anglia, the Cotswolds, Devon and elsewhere, and the spectacular steeple at Louth, Lincolnshire, the tallest of any English church, was built during 1501–15. However, all this came to an end in the 1530s when Henry VIII broke with Rome and declared himself head of the Church of England. All the monasteries were 'dissolved' and hundreds of their magnificent churches were razed to the ground. A number survived when they became parish churches (see chapters 3 and 4). For more than 100 years Englishmen's hands were turned more to destruction than construction. Parish churches as buildings were not greatly affected by this, but during the reign of Edward VI interiors were stripped of their 'popish' furnishings: statues, stained glass, altar fittings and chantry chapels where they existed. The seventeenth-century Cromwellian Commonwealth saw further determined destruction of interiors, although more than is commonly imagined managed to escape. Thus, the years 1550–1700 saw few new churches built in England.

By contrast, in Italy the years 1500–1700 saw architectural innovation and the building of churches on an unprecedented scale. This was inspired by the Renaissance, a new intellectual, spiritual and artistic spirit of the age. In the early Middle Ages Italy had never adopted the Gothic style as enthusiastically as France or England. In the early fifteenth century the Italian Renaissance or 'rebirth', centred at first in Florence, turned its back on the towers, spires and pointed arches of the Middle Ages and looked to the architecture of

its ancient Imperial Roman past. The ruins of this, the temples, basilicas (administrative halls), baths, colosseums and palaces, were visible everywhere in cities, towns and the countryside. New churches were a prominent part of a building campaign undertaken because the older churches were no longer acceptable to a generation of architects and artists inspired by the glories of antiquity which they had studied in situ and in ancient manuscripts.

One type of new church was a direct transition from the Roman pagan temple, where a rectangular building was fronted by a giant portico with columns, architrave and pediment. Decorative mouldings of antique designs replaced Gothic forms. Internally the rectangular ground plan lent itself to the existing tradition of a central nave and side aisles, but now these were separated by classical arcades of columns supporting either horizontal architraves or round-headed arches. The soaring pointed arches of former years were no more. The chancels and altars as places set apart for clergy continued to be placed at the east end. This was not the only model used. Centrally planned churches, circular or in the form of Greek (equal-sided) crosses, created a totally new kind of interior. Whatever the overall plan, buildings were designed according to the strict rules of proportion and symmetry laid down some 1,400 years previously. Domes were sometimes used, but not towers or spires, so that compared with Gothic churches, soaring heavenwards, Classical churches have a more earthbound character.

In the later sixteenth century architects of independent mind and imagination rebelled against the restraints imposed in the early Renaissance and created the much more dramatic, or melodramatic, Baroque style, where complexity, sinuosity of plan and voluptuous decoration characterised the exteriors, and dramatic spatial effects and illusions characterised the interiors. It was in Florence that the new architecture was born, but it was in Rome that it reached this Baroque climax. All these developments in Italy were to have an important bearing on English churches but not for some time.

In fact, Renaissance architecture first appeared in English churches not as the buildings themselves but in the monuments erected throughout the Elizabethan and Jacobean periods where recumbent or kneeling effigies were surrounded by huge architectural surrounds in multi-coloured marbles (see chapter 13). In the early seventeenth century Inigo Jones (1573–1672) was the pioneer of authentically Classical buildings in England, including St Paul's, Covent Garden, London, but he had few followers. The first major Classical church architecture in England was not early Renaissance but Baroque. Sir Christopher Wren (1632–1723) had visited Paris in 1665 where he saw some of the work of the genius of the Baroque style, Giovanni Lorenzo Bernini. After the Great Fire of London the following year, Wren was called upon for the rebuilding of St Paul's Cathedral and the City of London churches that had been destroyed. For these he was inspired to create his own version of the Baroque. Individually and collectively these buildings are the supreme contribution to English architecture (see chapter 14).

Throughout the eighteenth century the English gentry became familiar with developments in Europe while on their Grand Tours. They brought home the ideas that created their stately homes and the new churches in cities, villages (see chapter 15) and on their parkland estates (see chapters 16 and 17). When money was available these were built on the grandest scale with a columned entrance rising to the full height of the building. Inside aisles and naves were separated by columns supporting Classical arches or architraves. No expense was spared on the furnishings, which were now made from imported woods such as mahogany, lime and walnut. Pulpits, reredoses, altar rails and organ cases were carved by craftsmen of incomparable skill never since surpassed in England. For the congregations equally elegant box pews became fashionable and replaced simple benches. When there was not a great deal of money available, as in small rural villages where dilapidated medieval churches were being replaced, simple 'boxes' of brick with stone dressings, modest doorways and large clear glass windows were standard. Despite, or because

of, the lack of show the now mellowed brickwork and refined proportions make them among the most attractive churches today, and their interior woodwork is often of the best quality.

Apart from architecture and art, Georgian churches, both new buildings and those where alterations were made, were greatly different from their medieval predecessors. In the Middle Ages the mass (the Eucharist) was celebrated every day throughout the year. With churches having two or three priests, including the ubiquitous chantry priests, it might be celebrated several times a day. Consequently, the chancel was the most important part of the church, and as such it was reserved for the clergy and usually screened off from the nave by a rood screen. In the eighteenth century Anglican Church the ministry of the Word (preaching) took precedence over the ministry of the Sacrament and interiors were designed to reflect this. Tall three-decker pulpits dominated the nave, towering over the box pews which were positioned to focus on them and not the altar, so that the chancel became a relatively unimportant part of the church. Whitby Church, North Yorkshire, is the most astonishing of these 'auditory' churches (see chapter 20).

Despite the dominance of the Classical taste in the eighteenth century the evidence of a Gothic past was ever present in thousands of medieval churches, and most of the rural population would have been familiar with no other style. However, in the middle years of the century a small number of landed aristocrats became attached to a romantic idea of the Middle Ages, a mythical 'Merrie England', and an equally romantic idea of Gothic architecture. They created a fanciful 'Gothick' style where churches were liberally adorned with some Gothic motifs in a purely decorative, not structural, way. Shobdon, Herefordshire, is the most amazing example of this type of decoration (see chapter 18).

Towards the end of the century the success of the preaching of John and Charles Wesley led to the building of the first Methodist chapels as the movement broke away from the Established Church. Their number was soon to escalate and form a significant part of ecclesiastical building in the nineteenth century.

Compared with other periods of history, before and after, the eighteenth century saw a greater diversity of styles in church buildings: the calm classicism of the early Renaissance, the exuberance and drama of the Baroque, some reasonable approximations to true Gothic and the romantic fantasies of Gothick. All give pleasure today, each in their own way.

14
ST STEPHEN WALBROOK, CITY OF LONDON

Christopher Wren's Masterpiece for the Lord Mayors

THE CITY OF LONDON REFERS to the ancient 'Square Mile' which started as the walled Roman city and developed into the somewhat larger walled medieval city stretching from Temple Bar, west of St Paul's Cathedral, to the Tower of London in the east. Although it is now a centre of the international financial world it still retains much of its unique medieval system of government under the Lord Mayor, aldermen and livery companies, and happily it also retains many of its historic buildings. It is now of course only a tiny part of a much greater metropolis of almost nine million people.

On Saturday 1 September 1666 there were 108 parish churches in the City. By Wednesday 5 September only 21 were still intact. A fire that started in a bakery in Pudding Lane on the Saturday night raged for three days, blown by a stiff east wind through the narrow streets of mainly wooden houses and business premises. This 'Great Fire of London' destroyed St Paul's Cathedral, 87 churches, 13,000 houses and 14 guildhalls of the City's trade guilds or livery companies. An energetic rebuilding programme was led by King Charles II, parliament, the Lord Mayor and business people. The rebuilding of the houses, using more fire-resistant materials, was the first priority. That involved no great architectural skills, but the rebuilding of the cathedral, parish churches and public buildings was another matter. Fortunately, it was a case of 'cometh the hour, cometh the man'.

Left: A close-up view of the steeple. It is not the tallest of Wren's creations but it is the most intricately complex and playful. It is ingeniously devised of Classical elements assembled in a way that creates the same overall effect as the pre-Great Fire medieval Gothic steeples.

Opposite: Today Wren's City churches are hemmed in on all sides just as they were in his day. His tall steeples were consequently designed knowing that they would be the only parts of the buildings that would be clearly seen and admired.

The dome is relatively inconspicuous without, but it is a major feature within. The small building in matching white Portland stone built right into the angle of tower and nave was formerly a bank and is now a coffee bar. Such touching proximity illustrates the need to make use of every available space in the City where land prices are astronomical.

The man in 1666 was Christopher Wren (1632–1723), who is widely regarded as England's greatest architect. He came from a High Church family and was the son of a Wiltshire rector who became Dean of Windsor and had close connections to the royal court. Wren was 'a combination in one person of brilliant technical ingenuity with supreme artistic gifts'. He was educated at Westminster School and Wadham College, Oxford, and became a fellow of All Souls College there at the age of 21 and a professor of astronomy in London at 25. With other leading scientists he was a founder member of the Royal Society in 1661 and Savilian Professor of Astronomy at Oxford in the same year. By this time he had already become interested in architecture and in 1663 designed a new chapel for Pembroke College, Cambridge, and the Sheldonian Theatre in Oxford.

At the time of the Great Fire the style of the architectural establishments in Italy and France was Baroque. These were the two countries that had frequently led architectural innovation in Europe. The Baroque period had its beginnings in sixteenth-century Rome but came to full development in the seventeenth century, flourishing well into the eighteenth century in much of Europe. At the beginning of the fifteenth century early Renaissance Italian architecture had returned to the style and ideals of Rome in the first few centuries after Christ. The architects, at least initially, created buildings with cool, disciplined harmony and an elegance based on symmetry, well-defined rules of proportion and systems of decoration, using as their inspiration the ruins that could be seen all around. For over 100 years the perceived rules of antiquity were the only acceptable norm. After such a period it was inevitable that some of the more able artists would tire of, and rebel against, an established tradition that was regarded as somewhat suffocated by over-prescriptive rules. When such rebellion is fired by a free-ranging imagination the results may be spectacular, as they were in seventeenth-century Rome.

Baroque architecture (the word 'baroque' comes from the Portuguese term *borrocco* meaning a misshapen pearl) was at first almost exclusively confined to churches at a time when the Roman Catholic Church was going through a period of self-confident reform and renewal to combat the advance of North European Protestantism. The architecture that this reform inspired expressed itself with the same confident exuberance and theatrical drama — or melodrama.

Baroque used many of the elements of established Classical architecture but developed and combined them in novel ways, the hallmarks of which were complexity and ingenuity. Renaissance ground plans of simple squares, rectangles and circles were abandoned for complicated sinuous forms in which undulating surfaces, externally and internally, almost eliminated the right angle. Larger buildings were characterised by heavy massing, but Baroque could be done on a small scale as well. Interiors particularly were designed to give a sense of high theatre, with concealed lighting and illusionistic effects with no regard for the former Classical precepts and harmony. Structural surfaces were adorned with voluptuous decorative details. This melodrama extended to such things as statuary and the huge funerary monuments of the wealthy patrons who financed it all: popes, cardinals and the nobility. Two contemporaries, Giovanni Lorenzo Bernini (1598–1680) and Francesco Borromini (1599–1667) were the outstanding exponents of Roman Baroque architecture, the latter especially taking its spirit to the most extravagant extremes.

Wren never went to Rome to see the work there, but during a long visit to Paris in 1664–65 he saw outstanding Baroque buildings and was introduced to Bernini who was there producing some designs for the Louvre. Greatly impressed by what he saw, he brought the style to England for the rebuilding of the City of London. Wren continued the English tradition of modifying these foreign imports to

A typically Baroque ornament over the tower entrance: a scroll and festoon above an ellipse.

suit the national taste. His vision of Baroque for the City churches was different from that of its Italian creators. Wren was not interested in heavy massing, theatricality or voluptuousness for their own sakes but, as a mathematician with a flair for three-dimensional geometry, he was interested in the scope for structural ingenuity that the style offered. Geometry was a branch of mathematics that, as a believer, he considered to be the basis of the whole world and the manifestation of its Creator. As an artist he was interested in the varied decorative forms that could be used to adorn the geometry. His approach was more disciplined than that of the Italian masters and he wished to create a style that was a combination of the Baroque with the restrained classicism of the Renaissance.

In addition to St Paul's Cathedral, it was decided to rebuild just 51 of the 87 burnt-out churches, with Wren and his office to carry out most of the work, which took place from 1670 to 1720. This office necessarily developed into a large team of assistant architects (including his pupil Nicholas Hawksmoor), masons, stone carvers, plasterers, woodcarvers (including Grinling Gibbons) and glaziers. Wren pioneered the use of Portland Stone in the cathedral and parish churches. This fine-grained limestone from the Dorset coast was laid down in the Jurassic period, as were many of the limestones across southern and central England. Unlike them it is pure white, as it contains none of the iron oxides that give them a range of colours from pale cream to brown. It has proved a remarkably good choice, because the fine grain has resisted the erosive action of acidic substances such as the sulphur dioxide produced by the burning of coal in millions of houses and factories. Visually it is the brightest and most cheerful of stones.

The church of St Stephen Walbrook is adjacent to one of the major road intersections in the City where several main thoroughfares converge: Poultry, Threadneedle Street, Cornhill, Lombard Street, King William Street and Queen Victoria Street — their names reflect the medieval, post-medieval and modern City. From early morning to late at night on Monday to Friday the junction is a mêlée of swirling traffic. At weekends it is eerily quiet, as the City has few permanent residents. Within the circus created by the meeting of the streets can be seen a number of distinguished buildings: the Bank of England, built in 1792 by Sir John Soane with later additions; the 1753 Mansion House by George Dance, which is the official residence of the Lord Mayor of London; and the

Above: The interior from the entrance. A single photograph cannot show the ingenuity Wren used to combine longitudinally and centrally planned elements in the interior.

Opposite: The forest of Corinthian columns and architraves in the north-west corner that support the upper parts and the dome.

names) is only a few yards from the busy intersection but it is sufficiently distant that it has relative seclusion from the swirl of traffic. There was a Saxon church on the site which was succeeded by a Norman church in 1096. This was subsequently much rebuilt before it was destroyed in the fire of 1666.

In designing St Stephen Walbrook Wren faced considerable problems, ones he encountered with most of the other churches as well. The sites available were hemmed in by the newly rebuilt houses, they were irregular in shape, and they were accessed by streets as narrow as their medieval successors. (The king and government had earlier rejected Wren's plan to lay out the new City as a whole, with an overall master plan of wide avenues radiating from major buildings within circuses, the intervening spaces being filled with squares and residential streets on a grid pattern based on contemporary models of European cities.) As a result, in most cases the churches were separated from neighbouring buildings by, at most, the width of narrow alleyways; often the churches actually had to abut other buildings on two or even three sides – just as they continue to do today.

In looking at these churches now it is useful to understand three points about the way in which Wren overcame these problems to create great architecture. Firstly, Wren gave little attention to the exterior of the main bodies of the churches as they were mainly concealed. Secondly, he decided that the main impact of the exteriors should come from the parts above the rooflines of the houses, i.e. the steeples. Thirdly, the steeples apart, he devoted his technical skill and imagination to creating splendid interiors of a kind never seen in England before. In adopting this attitude to the exteriors Wren was effectively doing what the medieval builders had done. Contemporary drawings show the medieval skyline as a panorama of slender needles reaching to heaven, and Wren's work was deliberately designed to recreate that. It also created a paradox, since a medieval-style steeple with a square tower surmounted by an octagonal spire is alien to Classical architecture, which is not an aspiring architecture. Borromini had, however, produced a kind of Classical steeple on some of his Roman Baroque churches, and although Wren had not seen these in person, engraved pictures were available to him. Wren's genius is perfectly showcased in the skylines he provided for his churches. He included structures that were built up of multiple ascending stages whose elements were all Classical – including columns, round arches, pediments, architraves, cupolas

Royal Exchange, built in 1844, with its giant portico. In this financial centre of Britain the approach roads are lined with the headquarters of banks, insurance companies, investments houses and the like, dating from the mid-nineteenth century to the early twenty-first century. The latter are easily recognised by their towering walls of glass and metal, which contrast with the solid stonework of their Victorian and Edwardian counterparts. A number of narrower roads, mere alleyways which are survivals from the medieval city, are tucked in between their wider fellows.

One of these is Walbrook, which gets its name from one of the rivers or streams, now diverted underground, that run into the River Thames from higher ground to the north. The church of St Stephen Walbrook (always known in this form, which combines the dedication with the location, as do many of the City church and obelisks – but were assembled in such an ingenious fashion that when viewed from below or from a distance gave, and still give, the same overall effect as medieval Gothic steeples. This may be seen as an example of how the English never completely lost a sense of their Gothic past from their national consciousness, even in the most classical of periods. However, while Italian Baroque often favoured heavy voluptuousness, Wren's steeples are light, delicate and playful – the creations of a mathematician, a man of refinement rather than a creator of theatre.

The congestion around St Stephen Walbrook today is similar to that in Wren's day although the buildings are not of course the same. Today the north side of the church is separated from the rear of the Mansion House by a five-foot-wide alleyway. On the south side a similar alleyway leads to the eighteenth-century rectory, and on the other side of that rises a large 2009 office block in the most modern idiom – all glass and metal in a series of convex bays (replacing the more sedate earlier building shown in the photograph on page 116). So great is the modern demand for space that a low, two-storey building, formerly a bank but now a coffee bar, fills in the corner between the projecting tower-porch and the nave. The incongruity of this is lessened by its reticent design in the same white stone as the church. The body of St Stephen Walbrook was built in 1672–80, but the steeple was not added to the north-west tower until 1713–15. 'It is the most playful of the City church spires', wrote Pevsner. The steeple is recessed behind the tower balustrade, which has square urns. The lower stage is an open square supported at each corner by three columns, two of which project beyond them with their own little caps. Above this an entablature carries a similar, but smaller, structure, which in turn carries a delicately slim lantern of three tapering stages with a cross at the apex, an ensemble showing Wren's ingenuity and delicacy at its best. Much less prominent than the steeple is a green-coated dome further east, which is visible only from certain angles because of the surrounding buildings. Although it seems quite modest from outside, it is a major feature of the interior.

The main entrance from the street has typical Baroque decoration above, an oval window with garlands. The quiet modest exterior (except for the steeple) of this church in particular gives little indication of the grandeur, originality and complexity within. As the visitor enters at the west end of the nave the interior appears to have a relatively conventional ground plan, i.e. a rectangular nave flanked by two aisles separated from it by tall, slender Classical columns. This is the so-called longitudinal, or basilican, plan derived from the earliest churches of Christian Rome in the fourth century, which were in turn based on the pre-Christian basilicas that served as administrative halls. The plan was taken up in the Romanesque and Gothic periods in western Christendom and then again in the fifteenth-century Renaissance. However, the eastern churches of the Byzantine empire favoured centrally planned buildings, circular, polygonal or Greek crosses. These ground plans became popular with the Baroque architects of seventeenth-century Rome. At St Stephen Walbrook Wren cleverly combined the longitudinal and central plans as he did elsewhere in the City. Externally the simple rectangular ground plan seems to rule out any central planning, but Wren arranged the internal disposition of columns and architraves above them to give the impression of a nave crossed by two transepts about two-thirds of the way along its length, an ambiguity typical of Italian Baroque. The pseudo-crossing is covered by an impressive dome that dominates the interior space much more than it appears to from outside. The panels of its plaster coffering contain roses, laurels and palms, few of which are identical. They are lit by a small lantern at the apex. The placing of a circular dome over a square space below is accomplished in a most sophisticated way, unmatched in any of Wren's other parish churches. Eight slender columns, which also serve the nave and transepts, support diagonal architraves across the corners of the square, and above these are arches reaching to the base of the dome. In this Wren was rehearsing for the much larger dome of St Paul's, his pre-eminent contribution to the London skyline. Stained glass inserted in the nineteenth and twentieth centuries has been removed and replaced with a type of clear glass, thicker and less translucent than modern plate glass, that bathes the interior with a wonderfully cool diffused light that reflects off the white stone, the white plaster of the dome and the now highly polished buff-coloured marble floor. Such a bright interior was central to Wren's vision of a late seventeenth-century Anglican church. The 'dim religious light' of medieval churches might be suitable for the low murmur of the Roman mass recited in Latin by a priest at a distant altar, but it was not suitable for a Protestant 'auditory' church where the preaching of the Word was as important as the celebration of the Sacrament. The people must be able to see and hear the preacher and see and feel themselves as part of a congregation. However, for

Wren it went further than this: just as he considered geometry as the basis of the world and the manifestation of its Creator, so light made that geometry visible and represented the gift of reason from Him.

Despite this desire for light there is a striking contrast in Wren's churches between the white stonework and plasterwork and the dark wooden furnishings. He employed a highly skilled team of joiners and woodcarvers, including the master craftsman Grinling Gibbons, who worked with him over several decades at a time when such work reached an apogee of sumptuous ornateness in England. These men worked mainly in oak, which has now darkened naturally with age or by staining in later periods; a little lime and other woods provide variety. Architecture apart, the glory of the City churches is their woodwork. Here, St Stephen Walbrook, the lower walls are panelled in wood on which the arms of the Grocer's Company are carved at intervals. The grocers were patrons of the living at St Stephen Walbrook at the time of the Great Fire and were donors of most of the original furnishings. Their present company hall is a few hundred yards away alongside the Bank.

The greatest skills of the woodcarvers were always concentrated on the altar area, with its reredos and communion rails, the pulpits, fonts, organ galleries and door cases. The altar at St Stephen Walbrook is placed against the east wall without the projecting chancel of a medieval church, visibility replacing remoteness. The reredos is the standard tripartite structure with the commandments at the centre and the creed and Lord's prayer on either side, all inscribed in gilt. The borders are all adorned with the ubiquitous garlands and cherub heads, but over the Lord's prayer there is an exquisite bird in flight. The pulpit was naturally given pre-eminence in these auditory churches. A winding staircase with twisted balusters leads to the platform which is inlaid with decorated panels. A Classical column supports the tester, which has dancing putti and a heavy ogee dome. (Modern clergy generally avoid this dizzy height, preferring to preach at floor level closer to their listeners.) The font is stone but the cover is again dark oak, octagonal with twisted columns below, and around the top are seven small figures of the virtues and a twentieth-century figure of Christ. There is also metalwork displayed in the form of a ceremonial 1710 sword rest for the Lord Mayor on his official attendances, for this is the 'parish church' of the Mansion House next door and the Lord Mayors have traditionally been churchwardens.

The dome.
Left: The structure is panelled in stucco work and lit by an oculus in a small cupola above.

Above: A detail of the panelling, which is filled with floral and abstract mouldings. No two panels are alike.

Some of the exquisite furnishings from the Wren period. It was a time when such woodcarving reaching an apogee of perfection that has never been exceeded since.

Top left: The pulpit has a tall domed tester on which *putti* dance.

Top right: A wooden cover for the stone font. The lower panels have dancing figures surrounded by foliage while in the centre there is a frieze of garlands and, above, stand tiny figures of the seven virtues. A gilt crown sits at the apex.

Bottom left: The altar rails of twisted balusters.

Bottom right: A wall panel showing the arms of the Grocer's Company, patrons of the living.

In the church, there are no large free-standing monuments of the kind commonly inserted into medieval churches in the seventeenth and eighteenth centuries. This is fortunate because any such structures would interfere with the subtle spatial effects of Wren's architecture. There are, however, several hanging wall monuments, all quite small in deference to the architecture. On a column near to the altar is a monument to John Lilburne, 'Citizen and Grocer' who died in 1678. It has tiny figures of him and his wife in life at the bottom and a cadaver symbol of mortality at the top. On the north wall is the monument to Percival Gilbourne, 'pharmacator et mercartor', who died in 1694. It is another typically Baroque piece with urns surrounding his bust. These must have been erected shortly after the church was completed. Sir John Vanbrugh (1664–1726), the celebrated Baroque architect contemporary of Wren, is also buried here but strangely there is no monument.

While all of this is of the time of Wren there have been some changes. An 1886 restoration removed the box pews in the nave and bomb damage in 1940–41 was repaired after the war. There was a major restoration in 1978–87, spearheaded by Lord Palumbo, when the church had to be closed for a considerable amount of time. More than refurbishment and redecoration were required, as subsidence caused by the nearby underground streams had imperilled the whole structure. The foundations were strengthened, and with skill and ingenuity that Wren would surely have admired, a concrete ring was inserted above the top of the walls and above that a steel girdle, both invisible.

A radical reordering of the furnishings was more controversial. Use was made of the central aspect of Wren's plan to place a new, very prominent altar immediately beneath the dome. Lord Palumbo commissioned Henry Moore to create an irregularly rounded

structure in Travertine stone placed on a low circular dais. This was thought by some to destroy the 'longitudinal' aspect of Wren's space by interfering with the west–east sightline and with the walkway down the central aisle. Undoubtedly, however, most modern congregations prefer to be more closely associated with the priest officiating at the Eucharist in the way that this arrangement allows. Circular seating in light beechwood around the altar contrasts with the dark oak seen elsewhere. The beautiful original altar under the east window is now only an onlooker at modern services. It is proper that the spirit of succeeding generations should make itself felt in religious buildings that are ancient and beautiful but not museums, and this major work of our time is commemorated in an inscription in the west porch. This kind of renewal is reflected in what has happened and is happening immediately outside the City, where the present generation is dramatically replacing older commercial buildings that are no longer suitable for purpose and not always of any architectural distinction, while retaining hopefully the best and most historic of the past. The latter might be a Roman temple, a stretch of Roman wall, a medieval church or priory, grand or humble eighteenth-century houses or fine examples of Victorian engineering, all of which can be seen within five minutes' walk of St Stephen Walbrook.

Before concluding it should be recorded that those who minister and worship here are not solely concerned with their architectural inheritance, important as that might be. The Reverend Chad Varah, rector at the time of the recent restoration, founded the Samaritans, a telephone helpline for the depressed and suicidal and it operated from the crypt of the church for many years. Its work continues throughout the whole of Britain today.

Nikolaus Pevsner regarded the church as one of the hundred greatest buildings of England. John Summerson described it as one of the few churches in which the genius of Wren 'shines in full splendour' and John Betjeman, Poet Laureate and passionate lover of English churches, wrote of 'Wren's cheerful genius pervading the whole of the City even today'. Walbook is in a central area of the City less familiar to most tourists who prefer the area around St Paul's to the west and the Tower of London to the east. The relatively small trickle of visitors who come here will enjoy the experience every bit as much as the distinguished architectural critics quoted above.

Eighteen-century rest for the ceremonial sword carried before the Lord Mayor in procession when he attended his parish church.

15
ST LAWRENCE, MEREWORTH, KENT

A London Icon Recreated in a Rural Village

THE CHURCH OF ST MARTIN in the Fields is not the largest building in London's Trafalgar Square, but it is the most eye-catching because of its slender soaring spire and impressive Classical portico. The square itself is one of the great hubs of the city, particularly for tourists. A few minutes' walk away are the Houses of Parliament, Buckingham Palace (for which St Martin's is the parish church and contains a royal box) and several national museums; theatreland surrounds it on all sides. Thus, the church is seen by millions of people each year, and as the most photographed church in London it is regularly seen by millions more around the world.

St Martin's was designed by James Gibbs, a leading architect of the time, and was built in 1722–26. During that period enthusiasm for Classical architecture in England was well established both for churches and secular buildings. Fifty years previously Sir Christopher Wren had created his own individual take on the Roman Baroque style in the rebuilding of St Paul's Cathedral and the City parish churches after the Great Fire of 1666 (see chapter 14). In Classical architecture a Christian church is given the plan and elevation of a Roman or Greek temple, with a giant columned portico and

Left: Worshippers and visitors enter through the noble giant portico, which is semicircular with Tuscan (unfluted) columns.

Opposite: The church was built in 1744–46 using elements from several London churches, notably St Martin in the Fields, in its design. A steeple placed on the roof of a classically designed building based on a Roman temple is a complete contradiction in architectural terms, the heaven-pointing spirit of the former opposing the earthbound spirit of the latter. It illustrates the English reluctance to abandon a medieval past, even in a classical era. A churchyard like this is a haven for wildlife.

Opposite: The cool nobility of Palladian architecture is most evident in the two narrow side aisles.

pediment above as the entrance front. There is nothing above the roofline as temples are low, earthbound structures. This did not satisfy the taste of the English, who for centuries had been familiar with medieval Gothic towers and steeples. These had a symbolically spiritual function of pointing heavenwards to God and the practical function of revealing the position of a church on the skyline above the neighbouring houses or across the fields. Wren responded to this English need by providing his parish churches with spires, albeit with Classical rather than Gothic details. It was a curious contradiction that would have surprised and perhaps appalled the people of Imperial Rome and medieval England alike but it worked well in seventeenth- and eighteenth-century England where the strangeness of the contradiction became lessened by familiarity. James Gibbs adopted the same approach at St Martin's, where his original contributions were placing his steeple so that it appeared to sit astride the ridge of the nave roof

and constructing his portico with six giant columns in front of the west entrance. It proved popular, not only in London but elsewhere in England and Ireland and as far afield as North America, as the eighteenth-century colonists established their settlements.

The large, peaceful churchyard of St Lawrence in the village of Mereworth between Maidstone and Sevenoaks is a world away from the ceaseless hubbub in Trafalgar Square, but a first-time visitor might have a sense of déja vu. The essential features of Gibb's front elevation at St Martin's have clearly been copied here. The building of a new parish church in the eighteenth century in an English village is invariably due to the demolition of an older church. The parish structure of rural England had been unaltered since the thirteenth century and was to remain so until the nineteenth

Post-Reformation heraldic glass. Before the Reformation stained glass would feature bible scenes and portraits of the saints. The eighteenth century saw in a more secular age.

and twentieth centuries when it became necessary to create new parishes for expanding populations. Hence the appearance of new rural churches is invariably associated with the activities of the local aristocracy and gentry.

The Fane family came into possession of lands at Mereworth in 1574. Sir Francis Fane became fourteenth Lord Despencer through his mother in 1626 and was created 1st Earl of Westmoreland in 1642. During their Grand Tours of Italy and France in the years after 1700 the English landed gentry were astonished and impressed by the grand classical houses and country villas of their counterparts in those countries, which made their own medieval castles and Tudor manor houses look hopelessly inelegant and out of date. Returning home, they set out to sweep away the old and introduce the new all over England. They quickly became attached to the ideas and buildings of Andrew Palladio (1508–80), whose noble yet quiet dignity appealed to men of moderation, as they considered themselves to be. Colin Campbell (1676–1729), a Scottish architect, and his contemporary Robert Boyle, Earl of Burlington, were the leading and passionate advocates of Palladian architecture in England. John Fane, who would later become the seventh Earl of Westmoreland, commissioned Campbell to build a new house at Mereworth in 1722. Called Mereworth Castle, it was a replica of Palladio's Villa Rotunda at Vicenza in northern Italy. The earls have left the castle in recent times, but it remains one of the most outstanding pieces of early eighteenth-century domestic architecture in England.

Unfortunately, the old medieval parish church was inconveniently close to the seventh earl's house, and in 1744 he applied to the diocesan bishop for a faculty to demolish it and build a new church about half a mile away. This is the church we see today. Colin Campbell was dead by the time it was built and the architect of the new church is unknown. He was clearly familiar with St Martin's in Trafalgar Square. The steeple perched on the roof ridge is to Gibbs' plan and can be seen for miles around. The lower stage above the roof is a square tower giving way to an octagonal spire which has clocks on four of its faces. The octagon is topped with a balustrade and a slim obelisk tops the composition. The portico and corner stones of the body of the church are constructed of ashlar (finely cut) sandstone. The side walls are of Kentish Ragstone, a hard, coarse limestone that cannot be cut or coursed with the same degree of refinement but has been popular in a county with little good building stone. The entrance front is not an exact copy of St Martin's. The projecting portico here is semicircular, not straight. The ground plan of the church behind the tower is a simple rectangle. The side walls have plain, round-arched windows.

The interior has none of the imitative character of the exterior. In the post-Reformation Protestant tradition there is no division between nave and chancel. The broadness of the nave contrasts with the extreme narrowness of the aisles, from which it is separated by massive columns which carry a lintel rather than arches. The wide walls have attached half columns so that the aisles appear more as colonnaded passageways, where the austere simplicity of Palladian architecture is at its most overpowering in this interior. A west gallery was the Fane family pew.

Fane family monuments were transferred here from the old church. The most striking is that of Sir Thomas Fane and his wife, who died in 1589 and 1626 respectively. It was designed at a crossing point in both religious attitudes and art. The pre-Reformation sense of piety remains. The couple lie on a tomb chest and their sons kneel in front. All have their hands joined in prayer. How the monument differs from those of a generation earlier is the adoption of an elaborate architectural superstructure entirely in the classical Renaissance style, which came to England in monumental sculpture earlier than it did in architecture. Gilded angels hover above, welcoming the deceased into paradise. Also from the old church came several windows of heraldic glass relating to the Fane family and their aristocratic relations. This is clearly post-Reformation. Before then, the stained glass that filled medieval churches would have shown biblical scenes and the saints as aids to piety, though heraldic work could be incorporated in a minor way. A large quantity, but by no means all, of this type of glass was destroyed during the Reformation and was not to reappear until the Victorian era. Most of the original wooden furnishings have been removed. The pews of 1900 are of the standard type but St Lawrence's remains 'the outstanding eighteenth century church in the county in scale, ambition and architectural interest'.

Opposite: A monument to Sir Thomas Fane, who died in 1589, and his wife, who died in 1626. It comes from the original church in the village. They lie on a tomb with their sons kneeling below. Gilded angels above welcome them into heaven. At this time a spirit of medieval piety still prevailed but the surrounding architecture is of the Renaissance.

16

ST MICHAEL AND ALL ANGELS, GREAT WITLEY, WORCESTERSHIRE

A Georgian Church with a Unique Italian Interior

The vast ruins of Witley Court occupy the foreground. The tower of the church is seen in the left of the background. Both have undergone a long series of changes since the time of their medieval predecessors and the village that once surrounded the church has been moved. Since the photograph was taken the grounds have undergone extensive restoration.

THE VILLAGE OF GREAT WITLEY is on the rural western edge of Worcestershire near the Herefordshire border, about ten miles north-west of Worcester, where the approach roads cut through thickly wooded hills. The village and its parish church became separated nearly 300 years ago, when the parish church remained where it had been for about 600 years and the village moved to its present site about a mile away. An old church and a new church, an old house and a new house and two noble families are part of a long and evolving story.

In 1665 the village, its parish church and a Jacobean mansion called Witley Court were clustered together in the feudal fashion. The mansion was bought in that year

The vast ruins of Witley Court occupy the foreground. The tower of the church is seen in the left of the background. Both have undergone a long series of changes since the time of their medieval predecessors and the village that once surrounded the church has been moved. Since the photograph was taken the grounds have undergone extensive restoration.

The medieval parish church was demolished and rebuilt here, closer to the house, by the first Lord Foley in 1735 in a restrained Classical style. Although still the parish church it is some way from the modern village.

by Thomas Foley, the son of a wealthy iron worker from Stourbridge, an area that spearheaded the Industrial Revolution. Foley enlarged the already large house before he died in 1677. His son, Thomas II, continued to add to the family wealth and the magnificence of the house. The next Foley, Thomas III, succeeded in 1702. He was created the first Baron Foley by Queen Anne. He too continued work on the Court but his attention turned to the then dilapidated parish church, which was about 200 yards away to the side of the house. At a time when Gothic architecture had come to be widely despised, he decided to demolish the old church and build anew. At that time many great landowners took this sort of opportunity as an excuse to have the church removed out of sight of their houses for the sake of the privacy that had become increasingly important to the nobility. Lord Foley did the opposite and placed the new church closer to his house so that the west side of the latter and the east end of the church almost touch; it has often been mistaken by visitors for a private domestic chapel which it is not.

Thomas III died in 1733 before the church was completed. His widow and his heir, Thomas IV, the second Lord Foley, shared his vision and the new church was consecrated in 1735. During this period the villagers were 'persuaded' to move to the site of the present village, out of sight of the house. The fact that it was also out of sight of their parish church was not something that would have troubled people of Thomas' station.

In the early eighteenth century there was no question that the new church would be in the Classical style that was then being revived in every new building, ecclesiastical or secular, throughout England. Witley church was built of brick with stone dressings with the cool, grave undemonstrative classicism of the Palladian type favoured by the English aristocracy. The ground plan is a simple rectangle except for two shallowly projecting transepts at the east end. The round-headed windows have pilaster surrounds for emphasis and keystones above. The modest one-storey west porch has a single pair of columns and pediment. Above this is a square bell tower leading up to the only touch of the Baroque on the exterior, an open-arched cupola topped by an orb and a cross.

Inside one enters a wonderland — a wonderland not at all originally envisaged by Thomas III. Every

Opposite: The unique interior seen from the chancel, 'where you are transported into a different climate. Here is the most Italianate ecclesiastical space in the whole of England'. All the surface decorative work was transported from a ducal palace chapel near London.

square foot of wall is covered with gilt mouldings on a white background. The ceiling is also similarly covered, except where there are paintings. This is an entirely Baroque ensemble seen in no other English parish church. One might think of a state room in Versailles or some English palace such as Greenwich or Whitehall. Such decoration came to be here by an extraordinary set of circumstances. James Brydges was

Paymaster General to the military during the Wars of 1702–13, under the command of John Churchill, later first Duke of Marlborough. Although Brydges amassed a fortune through the corrupt allocation of contracts, he was created first Duke of Chandos by George I in 1719. Using the proceeds of his wartime dealings he built a palace at Canons, his estate in Edgware, north London, which included a substantial and sumptuously

Right: The largest of the paintings, the centrepiece of the nave ceiling shows the *Ascension of Christ* by Antonio Bellucci.

decorated chapel. (Marlborough had already started a palace at Blenheim on an even grander scale shortly before; it was paid for by Queen Anne.) Unfortunately for Chandos he lost much of his fortune in the South Sea Bubble of 1720 and was forced to sell up palace, contents and estate.

The second Lord Foley, being told that the Canons chapel was about the same size as his own at Witley Court, decided in 1747 to purchase all that was moveable, probably at a rock bottom price. Had this simply been woodwork, such as screens, reredos, pulpit, benches etc., there would have been no difficulty. However, the unique feature of the Chandos chapel was the decorative work attached to the architecture. At this time the aristocracy were employing Italian craftsmen, the most skilled of their kind, to come to England to decorate their new stately homes. The Canons chapel interior was clothed in ornate stucco (plaster) work by Pietro Bagutti and paintings by Antonio Bellucci. The painted windows were by contemporary leading English glaziers.

The transfer of all these halfway across England must have been a mammoth task. The windows would have been relatively easy to take out and reassemble. The paintings, which were on canvas, were possible to remove. The stucco work was of course impossible to move. An ingenious technique was devised to bring it to Witley. Mouldings of the work were made in *papier mâché*, a newly invented material, and these were sent north. The work was supervised by James Gibbs, the foremost Baroque architect then practising in England. He had trained in Rome and would have appreciated the quality of the work he was preserving. The fitting of work made to measure for one building into another, however similar, must have been a task requiring skill and endless patience, but in this instance only a few alterations were necessary. As already stated the stucco covers all the walls. The ceiling has no fewer than three large and 20 small paintings by Bellini, the main series being the Nativity, the Deposition from the Cross and the Ascension. In the fashion of the eighteenth century the coloured scenes in the windows were painted on the glass surface with a brush, as one would paint on canvas, and then fired in a kiln. The result is a pictorial effect quite different from that of windows from the Middle Ages and the later Gothic Revival where the colour is made part of the glass while it is molten.

Top: Embrasure above a window with medallions by Bellucci.

Right: Gilded wall decoration, pre-Rococo in style.

One of the eighteenth-century pictorial windows where the paint was applied to the surface and then fired. This method was in contrast to that used to make medieval stained glass where the colour was incorporated in the molten material. The scene is the Baptism of Christ in the River Jordan.

When the glass is cold, suitably cut pieces are assembled jigsaw style to make the picture.

When this extraordinary ensemble was completed, the second Lord Foley erected a monument to his father, the first lord who had conceived the church. It is one of the largest and finest of its kind in England, surpassing many of those in Westminster Abbey. The scale of the monument can be gauged from the height of the plinth, which alone is about six feet tall. The figures are in white marble and grouped around a grey obelisk. The earl is in a semi-reclining position, head in hands, gazing into the distance. His wife is shown grieving but composed at his side. Five children who predeceased their parents are arranged above and below them. Monuments on this scale, or approaching it, are far from rare in English country

Monument to the first Lord Foley by Rysbrack, *c*.1740. It is one of the largest funerary monuments in England and could compete with anything in Westminster Abbey.

Monument to Lord Foley (detail). He reclines on an elbow, gazing pensively into the distance. His wife mourns in a restrained manner with a child.

with stone, which was regarded as a more prestigious material, and for harmony the church was refaced in the same way. Ornate gardens were laid out with two fountains that rival those in Trafalgar Square in London. Beyond the gardens was a 1,000-acre deer park. The effect was not greatly less than that of Blenheim Palace. English and foreign royalty were entertained here on a regular basis. The Dudleys added some good-quality furnishings to the church, including a pulpit, font and new benches to replace the former box pews.

However, the fortunes of this family proved not impregnable either. By the 1890s foreign competition reduced the price of iron and coal. The First World War and the recession that followed finished their empire. The estate was again sold in 1920 to a Kidderminster businessman who attempted to maintain house and estate in a reasonable, if reduced, condition. However, a fire on a September evening in 1937 reduced half of the Court to a burnt-out shell. What was left was sold to contractors who cared only for the materials that could be stripped away and sold. Neglect and vandalism during the next 30 years completed the ruination.

churches near to stately homes. In Westminster Abbey such edifices are often surrounded by noisy crowds. In a place like this, one stands alone in silence gazing into a face while almost feeling some personal communication with the person behind the marble whose world and social position were so different from that of today's visitor.

This was not to be the end of events at Witley Court. In the early nineteenth century the Foley family fortunes were eroded by Thomas VII, an inveterate gambler, and the estate had to be sold. The new owners were the Ward family, Earls of Dudley. Like the Foleys they were Midlands industrialists with an even greater fortune based on coal, iron and limestone quarries. Witley Court, already an impressive mansion, was enlarged into a palace of staggering luxury. More wings were added, which were connected to the main block by sweeping quadrants. The Court was refaced

As the church was parochial it was not involved in any of the sales and escaped the fire and later depredation of the house, although without the support of a family in residence its condition gradually deteriorated. All old buildings require regular maintenance but in this case the extreme delicacy of the interior Baroque decoration was in much greater danger from the elements. In the 1960s a group of local people and supporters elsewhere began a long campaign to restore and protect this uniquely historic building. Their work continues to this day and is the reason why a church in good condition is in regular use for worship and other activities. English Heritage has taken over the care of the Court and the gardens. The former is and will remain a magnificent shell, its giant porticos leading to state rooms that now open to the sky. However, the gardens and fountains have been restored to some resemblance of their former glory.

17
ST MARGARET, WELL, LINCOLNSHIRE

A 'Roman Temple' as an Eye-catcher in a Stately Park

AT THE BEGINNING OF THE eighteenth century the English aristocracy and landed gentry were living in the same country seats that their families had occupied for generations. There were castles dating from the time of the Normans and many Tudor and Jacobean mansions. It became customary for the nobility to make the Grand Tour to Italy and France, where they saw that the houses of their counterparts there were very different from their own back home. The Italians had rejected the Gothic style of architecture in the early fifteenth century, in a classical Renaissance during which they turned to the architecture of Imperial Rome as the basis of all buildings, domestic and ecclesiastical. The stately homes or villas of the Italian aristocracy in town and country were planned according to the rules of symmetry

From the front of Well Hall, the parish church of St Margaret is seen as an eye-catcher in the form of a Roman temple.

The portico of the little church built in 1733, which faces the Hall, was modelled on that of St Paul's church, Covent Garden, London.

and proportion that they saw in the ruins of ancient buildings and in antique manuscripts. Noble entrance fronts had giant columned porticos surmounted by pediments, all with Classical decoration. These led into high marbled entrance halls with state rooms logically and symmetrically arranged around them. Compared with these edifices, the English castles and old mansions, impressive enough in their way, seemed hopelessly out of date as they lacked planning, elegance and convenient domestic arrangements. Therefore, demolition and rebuilding in England began on a large scale and continued throughout the century. The nobility and the leading architects they employed particularly favoured the cool, calm nobility of the work of Andrea Palladio (1508–80), leading to the English Palladian style.

At the same time the owners of these new houses turned their attention to the grounds around their homes, creating a look that is today quintessentially English. In the seventeenth century continental and English gardens that surrounded great houses and palaces were laid out in strictly formal geometrical patterns. Flower beds surrounded by low box hedges were contained within a grid of squares and rectangles, with straight avenues radiating from central features such as fountains and statues. The straight line and

the circle had total control. English people of taste and education had for some time been attracted by romantic landscape paintings showing idyllic rustic scenes of antiquity in which buildings, entire or ruined, were scattered within open and wild countryside populated by groups of labourers and leisured people. These paintings were an important inspiration for the spectacular replanning of the land around stately homes, where a new naturalistic type of parkland, totally different from the earlier formality, was created. The name of Lancelot 'Capability' Brown (1716–83) is associated more than any other with the creation of these parks, as he designed and worked on hundreds of properties over a period of 50 years. Initially, they were very private places to be enjoyed by the family and their guests; now they are enjoyed by millions of paying visitors every year. Typically one enters through elegant wrought-iron gates between majestic gateposts with lodges on either side. A curving driveway leads across expanses of grassland, with large trees growing singly or in groups, and with more extensive woods on a low hill in the distance. The surrounding land will rise and fall a little and shortly a serpentine lake will come into view, fed by a small river. A handsome stone bridge may take the driveway across the lake, and it is at this point that some carefully contrived curve will bring the

The interior has a collegiate arrangement with the pews facing across a central aisle and a central wall pulpit. All the woodwork and plasterwork are in the best refined Georgian taste.

Big House itself into view. Today the whole ensemble seems entirely the work of nature, as though the house had been gently inserted into a pre-existing landscape. In fact every feature – the trees, the undulations of the land, the river and the lake – was carefully planned by the designer and realised by a large army of workmen. These parks are not just an exercise in horticulture; they are one of the greatest English contributions to European art – the art of the Picturesque.

The introduction of architectural features into a park was important from the start. These could be minor features, such as statues and obelisks, but generally more substantial structures were desirable, ones that could be seen from the principal rooms of the house or from carefully selected viewpoints on walks in the park. As 'eye-catchers' such features would add an element of surprise and drama to the scene. Sometimes there was a ready-made feature, such as a medieval ruin – landowners in North Yorkshire made use of the extensive ruins of Fountains Abbey and Rievaulx Abbey. If genuine ruins were not available they could be manufactured: abbeys, castles and all kinds of 'follies'. If the owner wanted something more in tune with the Classical architecture of the house, he would

turn to ancient Rome or Greece, with the erection of a small replica temple – rectangular or circular with a handsome portico facing the house. Some parks, such as Stowe in Buckinghamshire, Rousham in Oxfordshire and Stourhead in Wiltshire, were provided with numerous features of this type.

There was another type of 'temple' that could be used as an eye-catcher. A number of landowners hit upon the idea of demolishing an ancient parish church, which was in the village or perhaps in the park itself, and creating in its place a 'temple church' in the new Palladian style, strategically placed so that it could be seen from the house. This had nothing to do with piety or the spiritual needs of the family or the local people. The idea of a new parish church isolated from the village it served, with no regard for the convenience of the people it served, seems extraordinary today. However, this was a time when a noble family reigned supreme in its locality. Episcopal permission would be easy to obtain, as senior clergy moved in the same closed circles as the aristocracy. The same inconvenience must apply to today's congregations, albeit lessened by the availability of cars. To compensate there is the joy of seeing a landscaped park in all seasons: the awakening of spring, high summer sunshine, autumn colour and winter snow.

Well Hall and church are in a village not far from the south Lincolnshire coast. One enters the park through Baroque gateposts and quickly comes to the house. It was built for the Bateman family in the early 1700s. It is a two-storey brick building with a hipped roof behind a parapet. In the Palladian way the decorative details are minimal.

The park is an outstanding example of the Picturesque. Immediately in front of the house a lake stretches away to meet steeply rising ground, where the principal *point du vue* from the main windows is apparently a replica Roman temple near the summit of the hill. However, this is actually the parish church of St Margaret built shortly after the house in 1733. It too is Palladian, with a portico of four columns and far projecting eaves, and was probably modelled on St Paul's church, Covent Garden, London, designed in 1638 by Inigo Jones. Looking out from the portico it can be seen that the facades of church and house are aligned.

The interior is a gem of Georgian church furnishings, since churches of this type were built by wealthy men of taste who had little regard for expense. Furthermore, since they and not the clergy were essentially in control throughout the nineteenth century, the churches escaped the drastic re-ordering of the interiors that was widespread throughout the Victorian period. The interior is a small, compact rectangle. It is amply lit by a large Venetian (tripartite) window that fills most of the east wall. The walls and ceiling are rendered in a pastel shade of ochre within white borders with a restrained use of delicate stucco work. This contrasts with the wealth of darker mahogany furnishings. The pews face the central gangway in the college-chapel fashion with which the patron may have become familiar as an undergraduate in an Oxbridge college. The three-decker pulpit with a tall tester is in the middle of the south side. It is an odd position since half the congregation have their backs to the preacher.

Well church and its setting give a fascinating insight into the taste, influence and wealth of the upper classes during their golden age.

The Hall, built *c.*1720, seen between two portico columns. The two facades, church and house, are exactly aligned for maximum effect.

18

ST JOHN THE EVANGELIST, SHOBDON, HEREFORDSHIRE

A Gothick Fantasy Church Replaces a Norman Masterpiece

SHOBDON IS A VILLAGE ON a quiet road leading to the Welsh border about four miles away. The surrounding countryside is typical of Herefordshire, with gently rolling hills, which are quite thickly wooded, and fertile valleys with fast-flowing rivers; everywhere there are fields and agriculture and no towns for miles.

It is perhaps misleading to describe any place or building as unique, as all too often one is referred to a similar place elsewhere. Nevertheless, in the context of English parish churches Shobdon is truly unique in the combination of its situation, the circumstances of its building and the church itself. At first sight the village appears to be without a church, but a high stone

At this distance the apparently medieval exterior of Shobdon church is deceptive. On closer inspection several details point to a later date.

The interior is a fantasy version of medieval Gothic, or 'Gothick' as it became known, a conception of mid-eighteenth-century romantics. It was built in 1752–56 for Viscount Bateman, who owned the large Shobdon Court in whose park the church stands. The blue and white colour scheme has been compared to the icing on a wedding cake.

wall bordering the main street and a pair of impressive gate piers suggest to the expert eye a church within a park. Shobdon is not unique in this respect. Separation of village and church for the convenience of wealthy landowners was not uncommon in the eighteenth century (see chapters 13 and 17). The uniqueness of Shobdon lies not in its idyllically peaceful parkland setting but in the remarkable architectural creativity of two wealthy and cultured men who lived about 600 years apart. In the early twelfth century the land at Shobdon was held by Oliver de Merlimond, from Hugh Mortimer of Wigmore Castle for whom he acted as High Steward. The Mortimers were among the most powerful of the Marcher Lords. Merlimond was one of the highly educated and well-travelled groups of men who sponsored the work of the Herefordshire School of Romanesque Sculpture at Kilpeck (see chapter 2)

and elsewhere. At Shobdon Merlimond built a typically small church which was probably the finest creation of the School, rivalling even Kilpeck in its varied subject matter and the quality of the carvings. Only a few weathered fragments of this remain, albeit in a highly unusual and picturesque setting. To see the reason for this it is necessary to leap forward by six centuries.

The Shobdon estate came into the possession of the Bateman family when it was bought in 1705 by Sir James Bateman, formerly Lord Mayor of London, Governor of the Bank of England and wealthy director of several companies. He rebuilt the former owner's Jacobean Hall on a grand scale in the new Classical Palladian style. It was sited only a few yards from the east end of Merlimond's church. A large quadrangular stable block was built close to the other end of the church so that the latter would have appeared as a

small outbuilding in this domestic complex, more akin to a private chapel than a parish church. Sir James had two sons, William and Richard. When William, the elder son, succeeded his father, he was elevated to the peerage as the first Viscount Bateman. William in turn was succeeded by his son John, the second Viscount, who had little interest in Shobdon and spent most of his time in London, leaving the running of the estate to his uncle, the Honourable Richard Bateman. It was he who made the unbelievable decision to demolish Merlimond's magnificent Norman church and replace it with something more up to date. It shows how poorly such early medieval architecture was regarded, even in educated eighteenth-century circles. It was a case of elegance despising what it regarded as unsophisticated, brutish and perhaps frightening architecture.

By the early eighteenth century the dominant taste in architecture in England had turned away from the Gothic to the Classical, a style that it adopted later than any other country in Europe. Nonetheless, the English never completely rejected the Gothic and in the early eighteenth century several distinguished architects such as Wren, Vanburgh and Hawksmoor did some Gothic work when the clients or the situations required it. However, in the mid-eighteenth century a small but influential aristocratic circle developed a more broadly based romantic nostalgia for an imagined 'Merrie England' of the Middle Ages and that, of course, was a Gothic England. In the mid-eighteenth century the leader of this taste was Horace Walpole (1717–97), the son of Robert Walpole, the prime minister. His writings enthusiastically

The nave seen from the chancel. The arches bear no relation to medieval Gothic structures.

Opposite: The furnishings are in the same fanciful style as the structure. The three-decker pulpit has the original 1756 velvet hangings. The lowest deck is in the form of a little stool for the parish clerk.

promoted a Gothic Revival style as did the very much admired and influential house he built for himself – Strawberry Hill House at Twickenham, Middlesex. This early example of Gothic Revival was typical of its kind, not a true structural gothic but one in which Gothic decorative elements were superficially added onto surfaces. The ogee (S-shaped) arch was a favourite, together with battlements, quatrefoils and pinnacles. Bright colours featured prominently so that the overall effect was artificial, make-believe, a light-hearted gaiety with none of the seriousness of the thirteenth and fourteenth centuries. It has become known as 'Gothick' to distinguish it from both the original medieval Gothic and the serious structural Gothic Revival of the Victorian period (see chapter 22). Despite its artificiality some admire its picturesqueness over the dull imitative mediocrity of some of the lesser Victorian architects. Richard Bateman was one of Walpole's London circle who was converted by him to the Gothick taste and he decided to rebuild Shobdon church in this novel way. Building took place in 1752–56; the architect is unknown.

The church now stands in the middle of the park, encircled by lawns and trees. It consists of an aisleless nave, chancel, north and south transepts and a low, squat west tower. At first sight it appears of indeterminate medieval date. A closer look raises questions; the silver-grey stone appears more recent, and the windows and west doorway into the tower have ogee hood-moulds which were seldom used externally in this way in the Middle Ages. The door to the tower leads into a cool, plain porch lined with a number of small wall monuments. The transition into the nave through a swing door is sudden and breathtaking. The first impression is of the architectural version of a wedding cake, where a mass of white icing surfaces are decorated with blue piping in delicate playful forms derived from medieval Gothic but which could never be mistaken for them. Walls, ceiling and pews are all brought into the scheme, the latter having their ends pierced with quatrefoils. At the east end the very short chancel is separated from the nave by three pendant ogee arches where the lack of supporting columns gives a sense of instability.

The arms of the Bateman family in a transept window.

To the left and right of the chancel the north and south transepts open off in the same way. The one on the south side contains the Bateman family pew, complete with fireplace and elegant contemporary chairs. In the north transept, there are benches for the servants without, needless to say, any fireplace. The transept windows contain the painted arms of the Batemans.

The most striking piece of furnishing is the three-decker pulpit. The bottom deck for the parish clerk is no more than a chair and a footstool and above that is the desk where the parson read the lesson. The pulpit proper from where he preached is higher again, with its own 'wine-glass' stem support and a sounding board above. The red velvet drapery is original.

The only non-contemporary and jarring feature in the church is the dark glass inserted into the east

The massive Norman font contrasts with everything else in the church. It was the only feature from the original church not demolished in the rebuilding. Four lions prowl around the stem.

chancel windows in 1907. It has now been decided that this intruder should be removed.

There are surprisingly few monuments in the church and all are modest. The eighteenth century was a time when the aristocracy liked to commemorate themselves in style in their parish churches. Here the finest example of such commemoration is a restrained wall monument for John Viscount Bateman, the second Viscount during whose reign the church was built. It is by the distinguished sculptor Joseph Nollekens (1737–1823) and contains a portrait medallion of the deceased.

Remarkably, Richard Bateman left the font of Merlimond's church in place. Perhaps parishioners — who together with generations of their family had been christened at it — objected to the removal of something so closely connected to their families. Four lions, the favourite animals of the Herefordshire School of Romanesque Sculpture, prowl around the bowl.

In the middle of the twentieth century the external structure and interior decoration of the church were in poor condition. This historically unique and important church in an isolated position has only a small congregation. Therefore, the Shobdon Church Preservation Trust, the National Churches Trust and influential patrons have all contributed to conservation work, which has been expertly planned and executed with respect to the church's historical integrity.

We can now return to the first part of the history of Shobdon church. When Bateman demolished Oliver de Merimond's church not everything was thrown away. In these churches, including Kilpeck, special thought and skill were lavished on their arches, such as those in doorways and those separating chancel from nave, and Bateman had these carefully dismantled. The land to the north of the church rises gently for about 500 yards to the summit of a hill. Here he re-erected the arches as an eye-catcher in the park, at a time when these things were fashionable in such places (see chapter 17). An avenue lined with oak trees was created to lead the eye up to these 'Shobdon Arches' as they are now known. The structure is too small to be seen effectively from the church or house so visitors take the pleasant walk up the avenue to see them.

The old church had two doorways, north and south, and Bateman separated each into two parts: tympanum upper part and side-columns. With the chancel arch these gave five elements, which he combined in a unique *cinque*-partite (five-part) composition with some additions of his own. There is too much sculpture on the arches to describe here and it is in poor condition

Above: The 'Shobdon Arches' were a number of outstanding pieces of sculpture from the Norman church that was demolished to make way for the Gothick creation. They were re-erected in a composite creation on rising ground at the end of an oak avenue, creating a parkland eye-catcher as was fashionable in eighteenth-century Picturesque landscaping.

Details from the Shobdon Arches:

Left: A seated Christ in Majesty with attendant angels formed the tympanum of a doorway.

Right: Columns and capitals of an arch capital eroded by weather.

due to the erosion caused by being in the open air for over 250 years. (The sculptures at Kilpeck have proved much more durable.) The seated figure of Christ in Majesty surrounded by flying angels on the tympanum of one of the side arches is just discernible. Scholars and stone experts have discussed at length what steps should be taken to protect the work from total destruction. Plaster casts of some of the arches were made for the Great Exhibition of 1851 at the Crystal Palace in London, and these are now displayed at the Victoria and Albert Museum. The contrast in condition of the original and the casts is striking.

The Batemans ran into serious financial difficulties in the late nineteenth century (the agricultural depression) and the early twentieth century (the First World War). When the last owner died without heir in 1931 the estate was sold, and the Big House was demolished in 1933. All that remains now around the church is a handsome set of gate piers that led to the house and the large four-sided stable block which overlooks the west end of the church.

It is true, therefore, to describe Shobdon as unique in the combination of so many diverse elements. Within the space of a few hundred yards we see the remains of Norman figure sculpture at its best, displayed as an eye-catcher in a Viscount's picturesque park, a church that takes Gothick fantasy to the extreme and a mansion that has all but disappeared. The eccentricity of the eighteenth-century aristocracy hangs heavily over this place.

19
ST THOMAS BECKET, FAIRFIELD, KENT

A Tiny Church Alone on a Marsh

THE FIRST SIGHT OF FAIRFIELD church is unforgettable even for those who are familiar with English churches in all their singularity. Romney Marsh is part of the south-west corner of Kent that borders the English Channel. The marsh is as flat as any landscape can be, and since much of it is at or below sea level flooding has always been a serious problem. In the Middle Ages it came into the ownership of the monks of Christ Church Cathedral and St Augustine's Abbey, both at Canterbury. They initiated a scheme of coastal defences to reduce the inflow of the tides and a network of dykes further inland for drainage. Saved from the sea, the soil deposited by rivers flowing from the South Downs produced thousands of acres of fertile grassland. Since the thirteenth century this has been the basis of a prosperous sheep farming industry and the animals are still a feature of the marsh today. Marshland

The tiny thirteenth-century church stands alone on Romney Marsh surrounded by grass, water, sheep and sky.

A close-up view of the east end shows the curved roofs as they sweep down almost to the ground. Cattle as well as sheep graze on the marsh.

wherever it is found, either here or in the Lincolnshire and Cambridgeshire Fens, has its own special appeal. Superficially bleak and empty, it has its own beauty. At eye level it is the grass, the dykes, the reeds and the sheep that create the mood. However, in land as flat as this it is the vastness of the skies that overpowers.

The parish of Fairfield is not particularly remote but its few buildings are sparsely scattered. There are no more than a dozen farmhouses and cottages in all, each scarcely in sight of its neighbours. Nineteenth- and twentieth-century censuses show that the population of the parish has always been well below 100. There is no evidence of a deserted medieval village. It has always been one of the least populated parishes in England.

The little parish church is as solitary as the homes it serves. It is accessed from the nearest road by a 400-yard path raised above the marsh on a man-made causeway. The marsh is well drained now, but in the past priest and worshippers had to arrive by rowing boat as old photographs prove. What churchyard there is merges

seamlessly into the marsh without boundary walls so that sheep and cattle can graze right up to the church. Despite its smallness — it is only 53 feet long — the building is quite prominent, partly because of the lack of neighbours and partly because its disproportionately high steep roof stands out on the skyline. Here in the diocese of Canterbury the church's dedication to archbishop Thomas Becket is connected to his murder, allegedly at the instigation of Henry II, in Canterbury Cathedral in 1170. He was canonised just three years later. The church may have been built not long after, although the first written reference was made in 1294. That original building was timber-framed with lathe and plaster in-fillings. The builders were probably aware that the dangers of flooding and subsidence did not justify a more permanent stone structure. In the event it has endured longer than they may have thought. In the eighteenth century the lathe and plaster were replaced by bricks. In 1913 W. D. Caröe, a leading architect of the time who was noted for his sensitive conservation of

Because of the church's low roof height the eighteenth-century three-decker pulpit is perforce not as high as some of its kind.

Opposite: The massive tie-beams of the roof are only a few feet above the eighteenth-century box pews, dark contrasting with light.

ancient buildings, carried out major work using original materials and construction techniques wherever possible. It was a total change from the drastic and destructive 'restorations' of his Victorian predecessors, who would have demolished and rebuilt according to their own personal tastes. The aisleless nave has a shingled west bellcote, perfectly proportioned for the building, and rather domestic-looking casement windows. The chancel is markedly lower.

If the exterior and its setting are memorable then the interior is equally so. In most churches the eye takes in the body of the church first and later moves upward to the roof. At Fairfield one is aware of the roof before anything else — not only aware of it but in contact with it, as the massive tie-beam at its base is only seven feet above the stone-flagged floor. Its lowness and its weight seem to crush the building and the people within. Caröe preserved all the eighteenth-century furnishings, which Victorian restorers would have swept away. Tall box pews are painted white, which helps to offset the limited light provided by the windows. The three-decker pulpit is adjacent to the pews. Even though it is relatively low compared with others of the period, any preachers here have their heads in the roof. Traces of a medieval rood screen remain but it is not surprising that there is nothing in the way of fine

monuments or other furnishings. The church simply as a building speaks eloquently for itself and for the fact that the Church in England in both the pre-Reformation and post-Reformation periods felt it was called to provide for even the smallest of rural communities.

As an ecclesiastical unit the parish and church of Fairfield cannot of course exist on its own today. Even in the Middle Ages it was served by a perpetual curate rather than a rector or vicar. In the entire nineteenth century only 170 baptisms and 22 marriages took place there. Today the parish is part of a team ministry, which is common throughout much of rural England. There are 14 medieval churches on the marsh, together with three preserved ruins. Some are almost as lonely as Fairfield; others are in villages or small coastal communities. Most of them are much bigger than Fairfield but in their own way they all have the same rustic marshland character. The cost of maintaining the fabric of these ancient buildings is enormous, and their people work together in the Romney Marsh Historic Churches Trust, which aims to generate interest in all the churches as a group and to raise funds for them. Its supporters come from far beyond the boundary of the marsh, inspired by the desire to see that these churches continue to be preserved long into the future.

155

20
ST MARY, WHITBY, NORTH YORKSHIRE

An Astonishing Georgian Interior

THE LITTLE PORT OF WHITBY is at the mouth of the River Esk, where it flows into the North Sea between high cliffs. There are outer and inner harbours lined with quays, traditionally used by the fishing industry but now also by the Scandinavian timber trade. Tourists attracted by the harbour, the sea and the North Yorkshire Moors inland are, of course,

also at the centre of town life. From the harbour the land rises up steeply on three sides, so steeply that at each level the houses seem to stand on the roofs of those immediately below. Whether seen from the harbour at sea level or from the cliff tops, they are a memorable sight. To first-time visitors the town may be reminiscent of similar places in Devon or Cornwall.

The view from West Cliff towards East Cliff. Between them is the small sheltered harbour where the houses climb up on the steep lanes. On the skyline the parish church (left) and the ruins of the abbey (right) look out over the North Sea.

The revealing difference is the rooftops – bright red tiles made from local clay are used at Whitby, dark blue local slate in Devon and Cornwall.

Equally memorable is the view across to the cliff on the east side, where two buildings a few hundred yards apart stand out alone on the skyline, presiding over the town and visible from most of it. The one closer to the sea is the original parish church of Whitby; the one further back is the ruined Whitby Abbey. The origins of the latter are far earlier than those of the church. It was founded by the redoubtable St Hilda in 657 for, unusually, both men and women. It holds a notable place in the history of the early English Church. At the time of its foundation the Saxon Kingdom of Northumbria had recently been converted to Christianity by the followers of St Augustine, who had

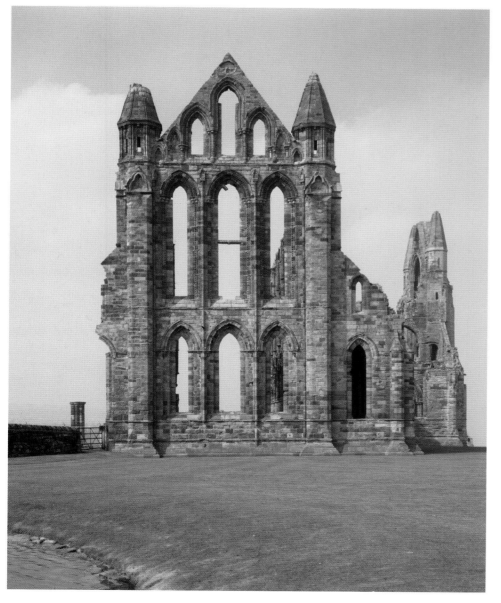

Like sightless eyes the thirteenth-century windows of the abbey church rise up in three tiers. The great Synod of Whitby, convened in 664, at the original Saxon abbey, was one of the most important events of the early Christian Church in England.

arrived in Kent in 597. The famous Synod (Council) of Whitby was held at the Abbey in 664 and brought together parties from the Celtic and Roman Churches, who were divided on the fixing of the date of Easter, the greatest festival in the Christian year. The Roman party led by the equally redoubtable St Wilfrid, later bishop of York, won the day. There are now no remains of the Saxon abbey above ground, although the plan is known from excavations. The abbey was rebuilt on a magnificent scale in 1220 but dissolved by Henry VIII in 1539, when it was leased to Richard Cholmley. We shall meet that name again inside the parish church. There is little left of the monks' domestic buildings but the roofless church stands up to its full height in many parts. The three tiers of Early English lancet windows in the east wall of the chancel now look out like a sightless man over the North Sea. They are one of the most moving images of destroyed English monasticism.

The church of St Mary lies between the abbey and the clifftop (towards which it gets ever closer as the friable sandstone crumbles into the sea). On all four sides there is an exceptionally large churchyard, crammed with eighteenth- and nineteenth-century gravestones which go right up to the cliff edge. From various points there are splendid views down to the harbour and out to sea. Church and gravestones are all of the same sombre dark buff sandstone. The body of the church is low and spreading; even the west tower has little skyward thrust. Perhaps height was not considered necessary in such an elevated position. Apart from its siting, the exterior of the building is not remarkable. It is essentially Norman from chancel to tower, as can been seen in the details of the doorways, windows and buttresses. The two transepts were built or extended in the eighteenth century. At the same time the nave was given a north aisle and rather domestic-looking large plain glass windows with small rectangular panes. At various points around the nave and transepts there are stairways leading up to doorways at first-floor level whose purpose is only apparent inside.

The first glimpse of the interior brings most visitors to an astonished halt. It is not necessary to describe the architecture in detail, only to say that the plain glass windows flood the church with light. The interest lies in the seating with which the Georgians crammed the building in the eighteenth century. Every square foot is occupied by box pews both at ground level and up above in all sorts of galleries. At both levels the pews

The parish church is essentially Norman with a thirteenth-century transept (right). Various Georgian touches followed later.

are raked steeply, as in an auditorium, and it is indeed a sense of theatre that pervades the whole interior. The seating was erected piecemeal over 50 years and no attempt was made at uniformity. Confusion and irregularity reign. The boxes vary considerably in height; some are at waist level, some rise above the head, making any occupants invisible. They are done to different designs in different woods.

At ground level the pews are fairly spacious and the gangways wide. Up in the galleries that cover the back of the nave, the whole of the north aisle and three sides of the south transept, the pews are more like benches with doors at the ends; the gangways where they exist are extremely narrow and become even more difficult to negotiate when the pew doors are opened. Access to the furthest parts of the galleries is only possible through the narrow boxes themselves. In a completely empty church it takes a slim and agile person two or three minutes to work their way from one of the galleries to the other.

The church is said to hold 2,000 people. However, modern fire and other regulations would not allow that number today. Once inside the purpose of the external stairways and doors referred to previously is apparent. They lead to prestigious pews in the galleries that are isolated from the lesser pews. The social distinctions and exclusivities of Georgian England were as rigidly maintained inside churches as outside. The nobility and gentry could enter, take part in the service and leave without coming into contact with people below their station. The most remarkable example of this segregation is the Cholmley family pew. The family were descendants of Richard Cholmley, who acquired the abbey from the crown after its dissolution. In the seventeenth century they constructed a pew in the form of a 'bridge' across the Norman chancel arch, thus making it, after the pulpit, the most prominent feature in the church. It is supported by four twisted barley sugar columns, all in white. The family left and entered through the stairway and door shown in the photograph below. Before the Reformation the rood screen carrying a large crucifix and the figures of the Virgin Mary and St John would have been in this position as a focus for everyone's attention. In that context the placing of a pew here seems an arrogance bordering on blasphemy today.

An outer stairway leads into a private gallery pew inside.

The significant fact about all these pews is that they focus not on an altar but on the tall three-decker pulpit which has a lower deck for the parish clerk, a second for the parson reading the prayers and the third for his preaching. In the eighteenth-century Church of England, preaching was paramount. The Christian Church in her liturgical worship has always exercised two ministries: that of the Sacrament and that of the Word (the Bible). The pre-Reformation Church emphasised the former; the post-Reformation Church stressed the latter in the form of preaching. The Eucharist or Holy Communion was in some churches celebrated only three or four times a year on 'Sacrament Sundays', and chancels, formerly the most important part of a church, fell into disuse. A weekly Communion Service was then considered a High Church practice. Matins and evensong were the principal services and at these the clergy preached at prodigious length. Sermons of an hour were commonplace, and two hours was not unknown. It is in this context that we must view the interior of Whitby church.

Thousands of medieval and post-medieval churches were filled with pews at the same time as Whitby, although not to the same extreme extent. In the middle years of the nineteenth century a greater awareness of the Anglican Church's Catholic past led to a revival of sacramental worship and a reduction in the amount of preaching. The Victorians also disliked box pews for the social distinctions they created in a church and for purely aesthetic reasons as well. As a result, box pews were gradually removed from the vast majority of churches and chancels were restored to their former importance.

The survival of a Georgian interior at Whitby is therefore remarkable. There is probably more than one reason for this. The cliff on which it and the abbey stand is too steep to be approached directly from the town by a road taking vehicles, horse-drawn or motorised. It can be approached directly only by 'Church Steps', all 199 of them, a considerable challenge even for the fit. Although today cars can make a circuitous detour out of town there was clearly a need for alternatives down in the town in the nineteenth century. In an age when an enthusiasm for church building prevailed no fewer than three were erected. Thus, St Mary's was less used but never abandoned and there was no pressing need to reorganise its unique interior.

Nikolaus Pevsner describes Whitby church as 'impossible not to love', 'incomparable' and 'one of the

Opposite: The first view when entering is an aisle lined with high box pews and a tall pulpit with tester. The white structure beyond with twisted columns is no less than a lordly pew constructed across the medieval chancel arch.

churches one is fondest of in the whole of England'. These are remarkable comments from a rather severe academic who saw and described in detail every church and secular building of any architectural value, however small, in every county of England, and who was rarely affected by such emotions.

It is to the credit of the Church of England that St Mary's has never been declared 'redundant' on purely utilitarian grounds, and so one of the town's most important links to the people of its past is preserved. The church is used regularly for services and other events during the summer months.

Above: An overall view of the interior taken from the pew across the chancel arch. Every part of the ground floor is filled with box pews, as are the galleries around all three sides, which are raked as in a theatre.

Right: The seating in the south transept. Although quite narrow it contains no fewer than three rows of bow pews at ground level and galleries around the three side walls above.

21
THE QUAKER MEETING HOUSE, COME-TO-GOOD, CORNWALL

A Simple Building for Simple Worship

GEORGE FOX (1624–91) WAS THE son of a Leicestershire weaver. While still a young man and an apprentice he felt called to a deeper and more personal faith in God than he saw in the churches around him. He left his job and home and travelled widely, debating faith and spirituality with Anglican and Presbyterian clergy while living in poverty. Shortly after this he received an 'inner light' during private meditation, and this very personal living contact with the Divine Spirit became central to his life. He felt compelled to preach this experience to others as he travelled across the length and breadth of the country and gained a considerably following, one that later spread to the new colonies in North America. Because he rejected the idea that Christianity should be mediated to a laity through bishops and priests, he was denounced, persecuted and imprisoned by an establishment that at that time could not accept any form of religious dissent. In 1667 Fox and his followers organised themselves into a group that they called the Society of Friends. Shortly afterwards they became known as Quakers, from Fox's exhortation for all to

From outside the simple cob and thatch building of 1710 might be taken for a farm worker's cottage. The section on the right was for worshippers' horses.
© John Blakeston

A section of the meeting room. Plain benches against panelled walls face a central table. There is a small gallery for a speaker at the other end. © John Blakeston

'quake at the word of the Lord'. It is a name that has persisted alongside the formal name of the society.

The Friends now required their own places of worship since Fox disliked the all-present parish churches, dismissing them as 'steeple houses'. Instead the Society set up meeting houses, and since the congregations were at first small and since any form of ritualism, visual aids or ornaments were rejected, the meeting houses were equally small and simple. Worship was unprogrammed, in contrast to the Anglican Church's prescribed pattern of the services in the Book of Common Prayer. Silence, prayer and meditation might result in one of the congregation, man or woman, speaking to the others of a spiritual light that they might have received.

Fox first came to Cornwall in 1656 and the 1710 meeting house at Come-to-Good in Cornwall is one of the Society's earliest. Come-to-Good is a hamlet in the parish of Feock, north of Falmouth on the wide sea inlet know as Carrick Roads. In addition to the meeting house there are just seven houses and one farmhouse. The unusual name was once through to be derived from the Celtic *Cwm-ty-Coit* — 'combe by the dwelling in the wood' — but since there is no reference to the name until *c*.1700 it is now thought to be simply an ironic reference to the meeting house. The outside of the meeting house appears as a cottage. It is built of whitewashed cob (a mixture of clay and straw) and has a thatched roof. There is a stable for the worshippers' horses on one side under the same roof as the house. It has its own burial ground but few headstones. Anglican clergy at the time usually opposed the burial of any form of dissenters within the graveyards of their parish churches. The meeting room inside is a simple panelled room with benches around the walls facing a central table. At one end there is a gallery supported by wooden pillars from which a person may address a meeting. An extension with modern facilities was added in 1967. In 1999 the building was elevated from Grade II* listed to Grade I. It is not only cathedrals, palaces and castles that gain this distinction. Architecture and age are not the only factors influencing the importance of a building in the nation's history.

Meetings are held at Come-to-Good every Sunday morning with a congregation of 10–20 people. Visitors are welcome Mondays to Saturdays and on Sundays if they come to join in worship.

Quaker meeting houses have never made their mark on the English landscape as have the 'steeple houses' of other denominations, nor have they ever set out to do so. Rather, Quakers have made their mark on English society for 300 years with their advocacy of tolerance and their historic campaigns against slavery, for penal reform and for social justice in every age.

CHURCHES IN THE REIGN OF QUEEN VICTORIA

Gothic Steeples and Towers Return to the English Skyline

IN THE SECOND QUARTER OF the nineteenth century ideas among churchmen about theology, church liturgy and architectural history were to change the appearance of English churches externally and internally for the next 150 years. Approximately 6,000 new churches were built during the reign of Queen Victoria, and these significantly altered the landscape, particularly the skylines of cities, towns and suburbs where most were built.

At Oxford University in the 1830s a number of Anglican clergymen were concerned about the increasing indifference to religion and the growth of other religious sects that was accompanying the Industrial Revolution. They were also concerned with the internal state of the Church of England. Since the time of Henry VIII this had always regarded itself as 'Catholic' in that it was the direct successor of the worldwide pre-Reformation church, and 'Protestant' in that it was a reformed church. The Oxford clergymen believed that its Catholic character was being gradually subordinated to its Protestant character. Thus the role of sacramental worship had been diminished by the growth of a mainly preaching ministry within the services of matins and evensong. In the eighteenth century new churches were built as auditoriums in which the pews were focussed on high, three-decker pulpits and not on the altar in the chancel as they would have been before the Reformation. The older medieval churches had been re-organised on the same lines. The Eucharist was celebrated as little as four times a year on 'Sacrament Sundays'. Chancels had become almost redundant. Anglican services had come to lack the colourful ceremony and drama of the services of the Roman Catholic Church, which had undergone a resurgence as a result of the Catholic Emancipation Acts.

The Oxford Movement as it came to be known was dedicated to steering the Church of England back to its Catholic roots. In parish churches whose 'Anglo-Catholic' clergy were sympathetic to the Oxford Movement, the Eucharist was now celebrated at least once a week so that the importance of the chancels was reinstated. Altars in marble or stone replaced wooden tables. Choir stalls and organs were installed as dignified liturgical music was called for. Vestments, candles and (daringly) the use of incense were introduced. At the same time the high pulpits were replaced by less prominent structures. These Victorian churchmen detested the box pews that had come to fill entire churches (see chapter 20) on several grounds. They prevented the sense of community that should exist within a Christian gathering. They were frequently oriented to face a pulpit, even if this meant that some of their occupants had their backs to the altar. Most of all, the new clergy hated the annual fees that box pew holders were obliged to pay for 'their' pews, often on a graduated scale depending on the position and size of the pew, just as in a theatre. Eventually, notices would appear on notice boards that all places in the church were 'free'. 'Free seats for all' was the rallying cry for the Incorporated Church Building Society, one of the National Churches Trust's predecessor charities, which was founded in 1818.

All of these reforms were enthusiastically supported by a group of undergraduates at Cambridge University, the Cambridge Camden Society, and their magazine

The Ecclesiologist became the arbiter of what were 'good' and 'bad' church furnishings. There was much opposition to these changes at first, as they were regarded as 'popery through the back door'. However, over the course of the century they became widely accepted and are almost universal today.

The Oxford Movement was concerned with the nature and manner of worship within churches. It was not concerned with whether the buildings themselves were Gothic in style or in the Classical style of the seventeenth and eighteenth centuries. It was, however, a matter of great concern to one man, Augustus Welby Northmore Pugin (1812–52), who more than any other at this time was to change the face of new churches, and many secular buildings, throughout England. He was the son of a skilled architectural draughtsman, a French Protestant who had emigrated to England. The father's meticulously accurate drawings of English medieval buildings had a profound effect on the son, who became a Roman Catholic in 1834. He developed a passionate, quite obsessive regard for the Middle Ages in both a religious and social context, believing that medieval Catholicism embodied the highest form of Christian spirituality and piety, of which Protestantism was a degraded form.

Socially the Middle Ages represented the perfect example of a true communal spirit and social morality, before the Industrial Revolution had created a selfish materialist society. Pugin translated these beliefs into architecture. In the Middle Ages the true Catholic faith and a high quality of communal life had produced Gothic architecture. For Pugin the link was inextricable: Gothic alone was the only acceptable form of Christian architecture, reflecting as it did the beneficent influence of the Catholic Church. For him Gothic was not a 'style' but a principle, a moral necessity. Classical architecture was pagan and earthbound. Pugin believed that Christian churches based on classical pagan temples as they had been in seventeenth and eighteenth England were an abomination and that the imitation 'Gothick' churches of the time (see chapter 18) were no better. Destruction, decay and irreverence were a result of the Reformation and the Renaissance, the former in religion, the latter in architecture. For Pugin religion and architecture were locked in 'unholy wedlock'. In his voluminous writings he campaigned fearlessly and

tirelessly to promote his views. Of course in all of this Pugin was viewing the Middle Ages through rose-coloured spectacles. It was not a time of social equality and social justice. Extremes of wealth and poverty existed side by side in a feudal society where brutal warfare and brutal punishments were endemic. The medieval church did not represent a perfect society either: corruption of many types was widespread.

From an architectural point of view many of Pugin's beliefs also made little sense. In describing Gothic as the only acceptable form of Christian architecture he was ignoring the fact that Gothic was created only in the twelfth century, after 800 years of church building using various Classical styles. The city of Rome, the heart of Catholicism, was full of Renaissance and Baroque churches. However, no doubt he had a point in describing Classical architecture as 'earthbound' in comparison to Gothic, which soared heavenwards. Understandable too was his insistence that a building had a moral worth that was more important than its aesthetic worth, and the value of a building was likely to be reflected in the moral worth of its designer. Pugin had a fellow champion in his love of Gothic – the influential writer and art critic John Ruskin (1819–1900).

Although Pugin used his new Catholic beliefs to support his argument for Gothic architecture, and despite the fact that unlike today relations between Roman Catholics and Anglicans were at best frosty and often openly antagonistic, his commitment to Gothic was enthusiastically supported, first by many High Church Anglicans, and later, more widely. *The Ecclesiologist* championed his views and all of the leading architects of the nineteenth century came on board the Gothic ship: George Gilbert Scott (and his family dynasty that followed), William Butterfield, G. E. Street, G. F. Bodley, J. L. Loughborough (see chapter 24) and many others.

As well as an advocate of Gothic architecture, Pugin was a talented architect and interior designer who worked prolifically throughout his short life, not only on churches but also on secular buildings. The most famous of the latter was, as a co-architect with Charles Barry, the Houses of Parliament, built 1840–45, where he was responsible for the decorative external work and most of the interior fittings and furnishings. The next chapter describes his finest and most historically important church.

22
ST GILES (ROMAN CATHOLIC), CHEADLE, STAFFORDSHIRE

The Spirit of the Middle Ages Splendidly Recreated

THE PIONEERING WORK OF THE architect and writer A. W. N. Pugin (1812–52) in returning church building to the Gothic style and spirit of the Middles Ages after a gap of some 300 years has been described in the previous section. He accepted commissions from both Anglican and Roman Catholic clients, but as a passionate Catholic convert his preference was for his own co-religionists. Since the various Catholic Emancipation Acts of 1790–1830, Catholics had been allowed to worship in public. There was a need to provide for native English recusants who hitherto had worshipped in private houses or carefully disguised chapels, and particularly for the growing numbers of Irish Catholic immigrants escaping famine at home. These immigrants came to represent a high proportion of the populations of places like Liverpool, Manchester, Birmingham and London. Unfortunately for Pugin, the financial resources of the Catholic clergy in these city slums were limited, so the work Pugin did for them had to be on a modest scale. He never compromised his commitment to building churches of quality constructed in a structurally honest Gothic style, but they had to be relatively restrained externally and internally. Seldom could he reproduce the ecclesiastical equivalent of the sort of work he

Opposite: Thousands of churches like this were created in the Middle Ages, but when this was completed in 1846 nothing similar had been built for over 300 years.

Left: The main west doors are filled with the arms of the Catholic 16th Earl of Shrewsbury who paid for the church.

had done with Charles Barry at the new Houses of Parliament over the period 1840–45.

There was, however, a small number of wealthy aristocratic families who had remained true to the 'Old Faith' since the Reformation and who were now anxious that their Church should once again establish itself in the public sphere. One of these was John Talbot, 16th Earl of Shrewsbury, who had both the passion and the wealth to support that aim. His predecessor, the 15th Earl, had established the family at Alton Towers in north Staffordshire, where between 1810 and 1852 he had created 'a fairytale castle

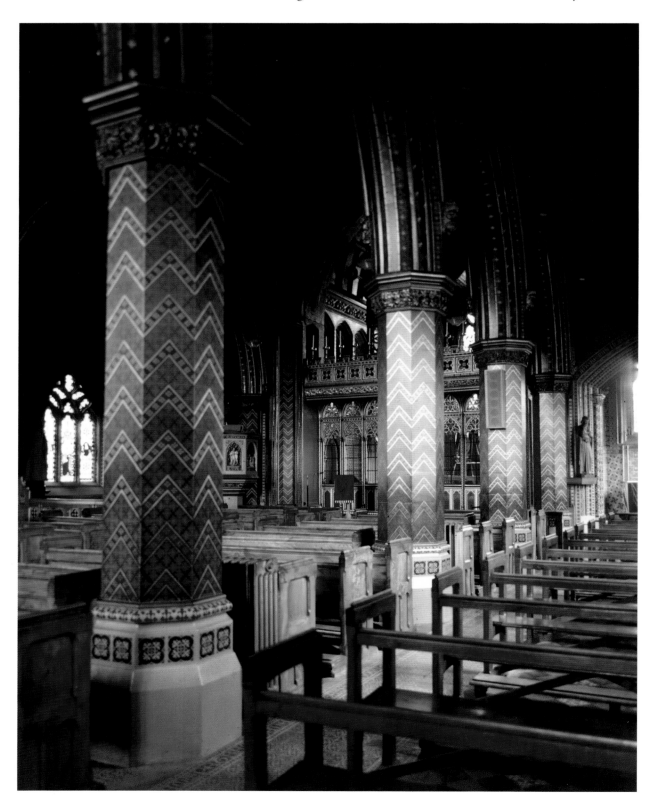

Like an architectural jewellery box, every part of the interior – roof, piers, screens and floors – are a blaze of colour. Every detail was designed by the architect of the building, A. W. N. Pugin.

perched on a precipitous rock on a scale of Ludwig II of Bavaria, beyond that of any of the castellated follies of other noblemen'. Alton Towers is now a burnt-out ruin and the earls have long gone, but the vast pleasure gardens intended for family and friends still continue to give pleasure.

Happily the earl's other creation has survived. When the town of Cheadle, a few miles to the west, needed a Catholic church, the earl stepped in and commissioned Pugin as the architect. Here at last Pugin was unconstrained by financial considerations and was able to build the church of his dreams. It is no accident

The rood screen dividing chancel from nave takes the form of its medieval predecessors.

that the church was prominently sited in the centre of the town with the west front adjacent to a main street. The days of backstreet Catholic chapels were over. It was undoubtedly a cheek, however, to have the church dedicated to St Giles, the same as the nearby Anglican parish church built a few years earlier. The arch-Catholic Pugin may have rejoiced that Catholicism was now at last squeezing out Protestantism, at least in the world of architecture.

Pugin had by then experimented with Early English Gothic, but this was a time when one Victorian art theory regarded styles as moving through three phases, from early immaturity to maturity and finally exhausted decline. In Gothic architecture these were represented by the Early English, Decorated and Perpendicular styles. Thus Decorated, often then known as Second Pointed, was the ideal. For Pugin Perpendicular had the added debasement of being too dangerously close to the hated early Renaissance of Tudor times. Accordingly, he designed a church that he described as 'a perfect revival of an English parish church of the time of Edward I'. Edward reigned from 1277 to 1313 and the forms used in the church are therefore the later, Flowing Decorated. Building took place during 1841–46. Pugin was not overly arrogant in describing it as 'perfect'. The tall 200-foot-high steeple can be seen for miles around, evoking the great steeples of the same period in the east midland counties, the aptly named steeple-chasing country. Pevsner describes it 'as one of the most perfect pieces of nineteenth century Gothic Revival architecture anywhere'. The needle-like spire has decorated pinnacles at two levels. The body of the church consists of an aisled nave and chancel with chapels. Buff carboniferous sandstone is used throughout. The west door has emblazoned on it two lions rampant, the heraldic arms of the Talbot family.

Inside the church is 'decorated wherever decoration can be found a place'. The nave is rather dark because there is no clerestory above the arcade, but the bright colours, predominantly red and gold, that fill the entire space (they are in the stencilling covering the walls, piers and roof and in the encaustic floor tiles) make up for that. The chancel is separated from the nave by an equally brightly painted screen complete with coving, parapet and rood above. The chancel itself is the highlight of the church in accordance with Pugin's Catholic view of the importance of the mass celebrated there. It is lit by a large five-light east window with flowing Decorated tracery. It has sedilia for three priests, piscina and a large Easter sepulchre, which was used in medieval churches for the reservation of the Blessed Sacrament between Good Friday and Easter Sunday. To the south of the chancel a chapel, in the same style, is separated from it by gilded wrought iron gates. Pugin also designed the brightly coloured marble font, to which he added an enormously high tapering wooden canopy reminiscent of those in late medieval churches in East Anglia and elsewhere. All this cost the earl £20,000 (about £2 million in current money). The church is not without its problems for modern congregations. A rood screen separating people and priest at mass is not in line with modern practice, and the overall decoration may go too far for some who may long for a respite by way of the cool, bare stonework of today's old village churches (although formerly they too would have had more colour).

The church was completed with the typically Catholic ensemble of presbytery, school and convent. The earl attended the opening ceremony, driving from Alton in an open landau watched by a large crowd – a display quite unprecedented for the Catholic Church just emerging from the shadows of the back streets of penal times. Many eminent churchmen and architects, Anglican as well as Catholic, visited the church in the following years as it became a benchmark for future Gothic church building. Apart from the Houses of Parliament the church is still regarded as Pugin's greatest creation. He certainly thought so, later writing, 'Cheadle, perfect Cheadle. Cheadle my consolation in all afflictions'. Affliction in the form of overwork and ill-health he certainly had. He died at the age of only 41, tired out, as his doctor recorded, by doing the work of three men by that time. His name remains pre-eminent in the annals of nineteenth-century art and architecture.

Top left: A view from the south chapel into the chancel.

Top right: The Easter Sepulchre in the chancel is also based on medieval precedent. The Blessed Sacrament was symbolically placed here from Good Friday to Easter Sunday.

Bottom left: The sedilia for the three priests required for the celebration of High Mass on solemn festivals.

Bottom right: The font is constructed of coloured marbles. Above it (not shown) is a tall tapering font cover of the type seen in some East Anglian churches today.

23
METHODIST CHAPEL OF ST JOHN, ST AUSTELL, CORNWALL

The Confident Assertion of a New Christian Group

JOHN AND CHARLES WESLEY, WHO were ordained clergy of the Church of England, broke away from the Establishment in the mid-eighteenth century to form an independent group with its own form of spirituality, organisation and government. Its members became known as Methodists – the name coming from John Wesley's insisting that there should be 'method' in the practice of private prayer. For a short time some worshipped in the open air in rural districts, but from the 1750s they began to build their own places of worship,

preferring the term 'chapel' to distinguish them from the Anglican parish churches. For much of the nineteenth and twentieth centuries people, particularly in country districts, would be described as 'church' or 'chapel'.

The preaching of the Wesleys was particularly well received in south-west England. In Cornwall over 700 chapels were built. There were large, church-sized buildings vying with the parish churches in the towns, smaller chapels in the villages and innumerable tiny, hut-sized buildings standing quite alone on roadsides

The impressive 1828 entrance front has a mixture of Gothic and Classical elements. The handsome portico came from a demolished local mansion.
© Chapel of St John

The interior was designed for congregations of 650 people accommodated at ground level and in an encircling oval gallery. The stage-like pulpit and the organ above represent the importance of preaching and music in Methodism. Many Evangelical Anglican churches of the time were designed in the same way. © Chapel of St John

between villages. As Methodism fragmented, splinter groups came to bear a variety of names inscribed on stones above the entrances: Wesleyan, Independent or Primitive. Many of the smaller places are no longer viable and have been converted into cottages but Methodism still remains strong in this part of England.

The chapel of St John in St Austell, near the south-east Cornish coast, is one of the largest outside of a city. It was built in 1828 and, therefore, is pre-Victorian by a few years. It seats 650 people, perhaps a quarter of the town's population at the time and still more than any other building in the town. The Methodist authorities were never involved in any kind of architectural wars between Gothic and Classical styles (see pages 164–165). A debate in the nineteenth century led the governing body to recommend beauty and perfection in design and execution without unnecessary ornament. The basic structures of most Methodist chapels were essentially astylar with simple rectangular ground plans without towers or steeples. Details such as windows and doors could be Gothic or Classical depending on local taste. The entrance front of St John's chapel is built of buff-coloured stone with granite dressings. The windows are in a late Tudor form of Gothic but the parapet has a triangular Classical centre. The handsome pillared entrance portico has a decidedly domestic look; it was taken from a local mansion when that was demolished.

The interior is as striking as any of its kind. Because of the importance of preaching in Methodism the pulpit resembles a small stage raised high on columns. A relatively small altar is placed in front beneath. The ground floor is occupied entirely by plain benches, and to accommodate the large congregations of the time a panelled oval gallery, supported on slender cast iron columns, runs around the interior. Music is also a prominent part of services and is represented by a grand organ in the gallery above the pulpit. All the woodwork is matching pine, attractively varnished and polished. Modern technology is represented by large screens above the pulpit. None of this plan is uniquely Methodist. As we have seen, eighteenth- and nineteenth-century Anglican Church interiors were designed as similarly galleried auditoriums for preaching to large congregations (see chapter 20). Apart from a different system of government Methodists and Evangelical Anglicans had much in common.

A chapel designed for the congregations of 200 years ago has problems today. Sunday attendance is low – about 50 attend – and those who come inevitably find it difficult to fund the maintenance costs. As a result, the National Churches Trust has made a significant grant. The chapel is, however, used for Methodist circuit meetings (20 chapels), concerts, music festivals and town carol services. The extensive ancillary rooms are used by community and social groups. The chapel council asserts bravely that 'we will continue to seek God's will for St John's and pray for His continued guidance and blessing'.

24
ST AGNES, SEFTON PARK, LIVERPOOL

A Thrilling Late Victorian Church for a Wealthy Stockbroker

THE SEFTON PARK AREA of Liverpool, located about three miles south-east of the city centre, was created in 1867 as both a park and an affluent residential suburb, when the council purchased over 200 acres of agricultural land from the Earl of Sefton to be laid out as an open space for the hundreds of thousands of people who lived in crowded slum conditions in the city centre. The idea was not to create

a conventional municipal park with large mown lawns and tidy flowerbeds, but rather something along the lines of Hyde Park and Regent's Park in London, where people could walk freely, play or picnic. A competition to design and lay out the park was won by the unusual

The church from the south-west, the smooth bright brick ablaze in the sunlight. The tall, narrow proportions are also characteristic of French churches of the thirteenth century.

Opposite: The church from the south-east showing the polygonal apse at the east end, a feature of French rather than English Gothic.

combination of a Frenchman, Edouard André, chief gardener to the city of Paris, and a Liverpudlian, Lewis Hornblower. André had helped in the design of the Bois de Boulogne in Paris and Hornblower in the laying out of the smaller, private Princes Park nearby in Liverpool. The flat, featureless land bought from the earl was made to rise and fall a little, trees were planted singly and in small and large groups, and existing streams were diverted to create a serpentine lake. The remaining land consisted of areas of natural grassland crossed by curving pathways. A little architecture was incorporated into the scheme and there are a number of grand entrances with lodges at various points. Within the park itself the finest architecture is the Palm House, a magnificent iron and glass conservatory now restored after years of dereliction. The cost of buying the land and converting

Opposite: The lofty cathedral-like nave. In contrast to the exterior it is entirely faced in stone with a splendid stone-vaulted roof.

Right: The chancel is surrounded by an ambulatory passage with much ornate carving.

177

it into a park in this way was offset by reserving land at the outer edges for sale as building plots for mansions and large villas which were themselves to be attractively integrated into the landscaping. From 1872 onwards this was the beginning of an area of grand houses, which then spread out from the park's boundary into spacious and leafy adjoining roads.

The growth of the new residential area led to the building of several churches, when wealthy patrons came forward to create buildings appropriate to their surroundings. One of those who had acquired a new residence here was H. Douglas Horsfall, a successful stockbroker from a High Church family, whose members between them built no fewer than seven mainly Anglo-Catholic churches in various parts of the city. He purchased a site in Ullet Road on the edge of the park and in 1883 commissioned John Loughborough Pearson (1817–97) to design a church.

Pearson was one of the most distinguished of the Gothic Revival architects of the late nineteenth century. At the time of this commission he was building the monumental St Augustine's church in Kilburn, London, and Truro Cathedral in Cornwall. Pearson favoured the earliest, thirteenth-century, style of Gothic, particularly the Gothic of northern France, the region in which Gothic had been created. The French style was for tall, narrow (i.e. spatially concentrated) churches. Early English Gothic, the style that evolved from it on this side of the Channel, was characterised by lower elevations and more spreading ground plans ('French soars, English spreads'). Pearson commonly combined elements of both in his designs. He had a unique ability to create ingenious and complex spatial effects in a church. These included the creation of receding vistas formed when one arcade of piers gave into another, which in turn opened into a transept, a chapel or an ambulatory. He realised more than any of his contemporaries that a stone rib-vaulted roof was literally and metaphorically the crowning glory of a Gothic church. It is an expensive feature to include in a church but Pearson was fortunate to design only for the wealthiest of clients – Horsfall in this instance payed £28,000 (about £2.3 million today) for the completion of St Agnes. Pearson was an example of the type of Victorian architect who combined his professional skills with a devout Christian faith. When commissioned to design a church he would retire to a short religious retreat, praying and receiving the Sacrament.

The first thing that strikes the visitor to St Agnes is its size, particularly its height and its smooth, bright red

brick. The effect of so much of this material is startling, and it is perhaps true to say that it is not so well regarded today as it was at the time it was built. Dark red sandstone is used for window and door dressings but hardly shows against the brighter brick. Its tallness contrasts with its narrowness in the French manner, and another example of this is the polygonal apse at the east ending of the chancel. The English style would have been lower and broader and the chancel would have had a straight ending. However, the projection of the two pairs of transepts near the east and west ends, a most unusual feature in a parish church, is in English Gothic style. English too are the tall, narrow lancet windows used singly or in twos, threes or fours. There is no tower (the building could scarcely take any extra height), only a flèche over the crossing of the nave and

The remarkable organ gallery creates a forest-like vista of columns when looking from the north-east transept into the chancel. It was an effect much liked by the architect, J. L. Pearson.

eastern transepts. It is flanked by two turrets a little further to the east.

The first things that hit the visitor on entering the building are the strong, sweet smell of the incense that is used regularly here and the relative dimness of the area where one at first stands, in a kind of lobby created by the gallery above. Typically of Pearson, even this is vaulted and separated from the nave by an arcade. Beyond this, in the nave, is the first surprise: the interior is entirely faced with a buff-coloured stone in contrast to the brick outside. This is surprising because most architects, today as then, would choose to reverse this: stone outside, brick within. The nave roof has a splendid stone rib-vault, something that gives the church the noble character of a small cathedral. The nave is not long, just four bays, with a continuous triforium (wall passage) above the piers and a clerestory above that. At the east end Pearson demonstrates his mastery of complex spatial effects in several places. The chancel has an ambulatory (a passageway with its own lower vaulted roof all around it) separated by a circle of piers with much rich carving above. To the south of the chancel is a Lady Chapel, with an aisle alongside the ambulatory. On the other side of the chancel in the north transept is the organ, which is integrated into the architecture by being mounted on an octagonal stone gallery supported by one central column and ten peripheral columns of black marble. This archetypal Pearson feature creates yet more vistas through a forest of columns towards the aisles and ambulatory. The furnishings are sumptuous, in keeping with all this spatial grandeur. The alabaster pulpit, carved with statues of Christ and the saints, is supported by marble columns and the font is of the same material. The altars and shrines around the church are exactly as they might be in a Roman Catholic church. Much of the rather dark glass is by C. E. Kempe, one of the most prolific of the late-Victorian glaziers.

By the time the church was completed in 1884, Liverpool had become a diocese in its own right. Consequently the church was consecrated by the first bishop, John Charles Ryle, on 21 January 1885.

Adjacent to the east end of the church is the red brick vicarage of 1885–87 by the noted domestic architect Norman Shaw. Pevsner says of St Agnes church, 'It is the noblest Victorian church in Liverpool' and it is doubtless one of the noblest in England.

No expense was spared in furnishing the church, as shown by the alabaster font and pulpit.

179

25

ST MARTIN, BRAMPTON, CUMBRIA

An Interior of Glowing Arts and Crafts Glass

Opposite: The 1878 church was designed by Philip Webb for the Howard family, Earls of Carlisle, in an Arts and Crafts version of traditional Gothic. Like most buildings in the town it is built of local red sandstone.

BRAMPTON IS A SMALL TOWN about ten miles north-east of Carlisle. Until the late twentieth century the main road between Carlisle and Hexham passed through the town but now it has been rerouted about a mile away. Shops, pubs, hotels and other businesses are grouped around a square in the centre, which is always an advantage in a small town, both visually and practically. There are also smaller squares and enclaves nearby, all linked by a network of narrow streets. Most of the sturdy-looking red sandstone buildings are from the seventeenth, eighteenth and early nineteenth centuries, all in harmony with each other and the surrounding countryside. The town has the typical North Country charm and character which is quite different from the softer prettiness of southern villages.

The late nineteenth-century parish church is the creation of a number of outstanding men of the time: an architect, artists and craftsmen, and a wealthy patron. It will be best to turn first to them and their ideas before seeing how these came to fruition in the church.

William Morris (1834–96) was the son of a successful businessman who had homes in London and Essex. As a youth and young man Morris had artistic leanings and he spent much of his time touring the village churches of Essex. He fell in love with the beauty and the quality of the craftsmanship that he saw and it left a lasting impression on him. He loved the buildings themselves; the carving of the stonework; the medieval tiles; the woodwork of roofs, screens and benches; the metalwork; and the stained glass. He admired the same sort of craftsmanship that he saw in the old farmhouses and cottages of the area. He contrasted this with the ugliness of their mass-produced contemporary counterparts, machine-made in factories by bored and dispirited employees who played little or no part in their design or construction. He became convinced that things of beauty and lasting quality could be produced only by craftsmen whose pride and joy in their skills was infused into the handmade things they created. He was later to become a founding father of the Arts and Crafts Movement, which was based on these ideas, and he was also the inspiration for other organisations that tried to improve design and craftsmanship and inspire the love of art. He believed that the creation of craft guilds of the type common in the Middle Ages would enable furniture and other craft goods to be available not only to the rich but to all classes of society. This view of the Middle Ages was no doubt idealised, as was the idea that quality, hand-crafted furnishings could be produced at prices that working class people could afford – hardly true even today, even with our higher living standards. It is interesting to note in a book about churches that Morris was the founder of the Society for the Protection of Ancient Buildings (SPAB), which was set up to try to stop the wholesale and damaging 'restorations' of old churches referred to in the Introduction.

At Oxford University he met Edward Burne-Jones (1838–98), a fellow divinity student. They became lifelong friends and working partners. Under the influence of Morris, Burne-Jones became interested in art, but while at that time Morris was primarily interested in architecture, Burne-Jones turned to painting. After leaving university Morris became apprenticed to G. E. Street, a leading architect, and

Above: St Dorothy and St George (in remarkable pink) commemorate Dorothy and George Howard, who financed the building of the church.

Opposite top: The Old Testament figures. Left to right: Jeremiah, Daniel, Solomon and Elias.

Opposite bottom: The New Testament figures. Left to right: Saints Peter, Paul, John and Luke.

of the Pre-Raphaelites had a sharply focussed, almost photographic, quality expressed in bright colours. It was admired by some and hated by others.

Burne-Jones was greatly influenced by the Pre-Raphaelite ideas. Following them, he favoured romanticised medieval and mythological subjects. In his own words he saw a picture as a 'beautiful romantic dream'. His pictures were peopled with almost impossibly fine-featured, nobly chivalrous men and divinely beautiful women. It was ironic that this style originated in a movement dedicated to realism. After their apprenticeships Burne-Jones was to remain a painter, illustrator and designer, but Morris turned away from architecture as such and instead took an interest in a variety of associated crafts. Dismayed by the lack of good craftsmen in every branch of furnishing, he became skilled in the making of furniture, glass, tiles, wallpaper and soft furnishings such as carpets, curtains and upholstery. He founded a firm that eventually became known as Morris & Co., and was based on the medieval trade guilds in which enthusiastic and dedicated men developed their skills. Pevsner wrote that 'this event marks the beginning of a new era in Western art'.

The company thrived, partly because of the quality of the very varied products it made and partly because of Morris' business acumen. Burne-Jones became a member of the company, producing some superb designs, particularly for stained glass and tapestries. Morris & Co. had no definite policy regarding 'style', but because of their admiration for the Middle Ages their work was medieval in character. There was only one full-time professional architect closely associated with Morris & Co. This was Philip Webb (1831–1915), who like Morris had trained in the office of G. E. Street and shared his Arts and Crafts ideals.

Throughout Victoria's reign new churches were being built at an unprecedented rate, especially in cities and their expanding suburbs. For these, stained glass was needed in large quantities. Since the beginning of the nineteenth century and the Gothic Revival in architecture some outstanding stained glass designers had emerged, including the 'father' of the Gothic Revival, A. W. N. Pugin. However, the bulk of the glass produced was poor. The subject matter was sentimental, and the designs were weak and over-detailed, as though they were paintings on canvas. The colours were dull, with much use of muddy olive greens and yellows. Like most other crafts at the time production was on a factory-line basis.

Burne-Jones became apprenticed to Dante Gabriel Rossetti (1828–82). In 1848 Rossetti had been one of the founding members of the Pre-Raphaelite Brotherhood together with John Everett Millais and William Holman Hunt. The name of this 'brotherhood' derived from their belief that from the time of the Italian painter Raphael (1483–1520) the art of painting had become debased by a desire for grandeur, showiness and false effects, later to be known as the 'grand manner'. The brotherhood believed that this had become ingrained in the aesthetic canons of the national art academies of Europe ever since. They considered that 'truth', or pictorial reality, had been sacrificed to beauty and advocated a return to a style of greater naturalness and realism that was characteristic of Italian painters of the fourteenth and fifteenth centuries. The paintings

Morris & Co. were to make the most important and individual contribution to transforming the design (Burne-Jones) and manufacture (Morris) of stained glass in the nineteenth century. Burne-Jones did the drawings (or cartoons) in monochrome in the Pre-Raphaelite manner, with his angels and saints having that ethereal, romantic quality so beloved by the brotherhood. Morris chose the colour scheme and supervised the cutting and assembling of the glass pieces. In the latter process he realised, as the medieval glassmakers had centuries earlier, the importance of the lead strips (calms) that hold together the small individual pieces of glass depicting such things as the heads, shoulders and arms of the figures in the picture. The calms create sharp black defining outlines and are an essential characteristic of medieval glass, which is so different from a painting on paper or the glass painting technique of the eighteenth century (see chapter 16).

We can now return to Brampton. Until 1874 the town had no worthy parish church and it was decided that year to provide something appropriate. The town was fortunate in this respect to be within the fiefdom of the Howard family, Earls of Carlisle, whose ancestral seat is Naworth Castle a few miles away. The family inherited the castle when they married into the Dacre family in the late sixteenth century. (The Howards of Castle Howard in North Yorkshire, which was made famous by television's *Brideshead Revisited*, are a junior branch of the family.) Members of the Naworth Castle family financed the building of a new church at Brampton and they commissioned as architect Philip Webb, a man who had worked for them on previous projects. He could design in any style but generally favoured 'free' forms of Gothic of any period without ever attempting mere imitation of the medieval. The church he designed for Brampton, which was built of the region's New Red Sandstone, reflects that preference and individualism. It consists of chancel, nave, two aisles and a west tower with a small lead spire. This description is a considerable simplification because the plan is one of some complexity. There is much inventiveness in all the details.

Brampton holds what is arguably the most outstanding collection of Arts and Craft glass in England. It was made by Morris & Co. (i.e. by Burne-Jones and Morris) and inserted between 1880 and

Above: Allegorical figures representing the cardinal virtues: Hope, Charity and Faith.

Right: The 'Paradise Window' filled with angels.

Two of three windows commemorating Bessie Howard, who died aged four months in 1883.

Left: The infant John the Baptist and St Elizabeth (above). Salome with James and John (below).

Right: Christ blessing a group of children.

1895. Webb had suggested to the Howards that the firm should be employed to insert the glass in his church, regarding them, rightly, as the leading glaziers of the time. George Howard, the ninth Earl of Carlisle, was in any event a patron of the Pre-Raphaelites and a personal friend of Burne-Jones and Morris. Morris in his turn was always especially keen to have his glass featured in a contemporary church rather than in a medieval one, because he was always fearful that in the latter case it would be part of one of the restorations that, as an SPAB man, he deplored. The glass was not placed here as part of one single overall scheme but gradually over the 15-year period. What the glass lacks as a unified scheme it gains in variety of subject matter. Like all of the firm's work it has a beautiful, glowing, jewel-like quality. It is all figurative glass, much of it commemorative in purpose, mainly for members of the Howard family.

There are 14 windows (many of them with several separate lights) by Morris & Co., a selection of which are shown here. The largest single composition is the five-light east window. In the top tier is the Good Shepherd at the centre and angels left and right. Below is a row of angels and below that again a row of saints. The latter include St Dorothy and a remarkable St George in various shades of pink. They commemorate

Dorothy and George Howard. The Old Testament is represented by the prophets Jeremiah and Daniel. The 'paradise window' is a rose window of angels. A window in the chancel has allegorical female figures representing Hope, Faith and Charity. Little Bessie Howard, who died aged four months in 1883, when infant mortality was high, is commemorated by no fewer than three windows. One of them shows children of the New Testament and their parents. Hundreds of churches have one or two windows by Morris & Co.; only a small handful have a complete collection like this as it was something that only the richest of patrons could afford.

When Edward Burne-Jones and William Morris died at the end of the nineteenth century a few of their followers continued their style and ideals into the twentieth century, but essentially their art died with them. The years of their work, therefore, represent a unique era in the art of stained glass making. Fortunately, the last third of the twentieth century saw a notable resurgence in the art, with a dozen or more practitioners creating pictorial and abstract glass of the highest quality in cathedrals and parish churches (see chapter 26). Invariably they use deep glowing colours that owe much to Burne-Jones and Morris. The desire to beautify the House of God continues.

THE MODERN AGE

IN THE DECADES AFTER THE death of Queen Victoria in 1901 new churches continued to be built in the Gothic Revival style. Architects like Ninian Comper (1864–1961) continued the tradition of the Beauty of Holiness in exquisite interiors inspired by A. W. N. Pugin (see chapter 22). Before the First World War the Arts and Crafts Movement (see chapter 25) led to buildings still being constructed in the Gothic tradition but being characterised by cleaner lines less influenced by precedent. Gothic adapted to modernity also characterised the few churches of quality of the inter-war years. Decades of austerity could hardly justify church building on the Victorian scale, much of which had been financed by wealthy patrons. This austerity did not greatly change in the years immediately following the Second World War.

It was different in mainland Europe and the Americas, where from the 1920s onwards architects produced churches of breath-taking originality with no reference to the past. These architects included Gaudi in Spain, Le Corbusier in France, Frank Lloyd Wright in the USA, Aalti in Finland, Mies van der Rohe in Germany and Niemayer in Brazil.

Little of this innovation touched the traditional tastes of English church people, but in the 1960s it became impossible to continue the now tired Gothic tradition. Furthermore, the birth of the 'Liturgical Movement' called for a different planning of new churches. The idea of clergy remotely separated from congregations at one end of a long church was rejected in favour of minister and people more closely connected around an altar for the celebration of the Eucharist. Architecturally, this called for 'centrally planned' churches with an altar visible and close to all present. Most modern churches now meet this requirement with handsome modern (but not

In most places today there is no need for new churches, so the efforts of modern church people are directed to contributions in the way of contemporary works of art that reflect the spirit and faith of the late twentieth and early twenty-first centuries.

Right: A crucifixion by Josefina da Vasconcellos in the thirteenth-century church at Greystoke, Cumbria.

Many churches that were the sites of medieval pilgrimages have restored their shrines destroyed at the time of the Reformation. At Beverley Minster, the former shrine of the founder of the Saxon church, St John of Beverley, is now marked by Helen Whittaker's *Pilgrims*, a bronze showing hooded medieval pilgrims bent and weary on the road to the shrine.

necessarily modernist) exteriors and contemporary welcoming interiors, where they serve those from modern housing estates or expanding suburbs.

Our own time does not call, however, for church building on the medieval or Victorian scales, but church people continue to commission artists to provide furnishings to reflect the spirit of our own time in thousands of ancient buildings which, as we have seen already, contain a wide range of works of art spanning several centuries. In an old church one may now see the best of modern artists in stone sculpture, stained glass, woodwork, metalwork, paintings and textiles and their contributions equal anything from the past. The late twentieth and early twenty-first centuries will leave their mark on churches as distinctively as in previous periods of history.

26
ST MARY (ROMAN CATHOLIC), LEYLAND, LANCASHIRE

A Modern Church with Ancient Precedents

LEYLAND IS A TOWN ABOUT five miles south of Preston. Although open countryside is only a few minutes drive away from its centre, it has the character of a suburb rather than that of a country town. Modern estate houses far outnumber anything from an earlier period. The Roman Catholic parish of Leyland has been served by the Benedictine monks of Ampleforth Abbey in North Yorkshire for several generations. When in the 1950s it became necessary to replace an older church, priests of the Benedictine order could call upon 1,500 years' experience of traditional and innovative church building throughout Europe. At that time they were also in the forefront of liturgical reform aimed at the needs of modern congregations,

The circular church built in 1962 is an early example of modern central planning. The detached campanile has an open concrete frame. The church has been judged one of the best designs of modern times.

The high altar with a corona above is at the centre of the church. The benches are raked upwards towards the back.

so a safe traditionalism was probably never an option for the new Leyland church. The then parish priest travelled Europe to see what was being created there by architects who were more innovative than their contemporaries in Britain. He came back with ideas for a 'centrally planned' church, in which the high altar would be at the middle. That plan is commonplace now, but then it was considered a startling and even irreverent idea by worshippers who were used to 'longitudinally planned' churches, in which the altar was set apart at one end and the congregation faced it in front.

In fact, it was not as new an idea as many imagined. The earliest Christian churches in fourth-century Rome after the emperor Constantine legalised the faith were longitudinal because they were based on basilicas – secular Roman administrative buildings. They had a rectangular ground plan with aisles on either side of a central space and a semicircular apse at one end for a presiding official. The latter became the chancels of the new churches and were occupied by presiding priests. However, some of the early churches used for special purposes, such as baptisteries or mausoleum chapels, were circular or polygonal. When the Roman empire divided into two in the late fourth century the capital of the western half was established at Ravenna in northern Italy. In the sixth century some of its most important churches were octagonal or shaped like Greek (equal sided) crosses. Churches in the eastern Byzantium empire, based on the then Constantinople, were generally centrally planned and these included the greatest of them all, Hagia Sophia in the city itself. Much later sixteenth- and seventeenth-century churches of the Italian Renaissance were commonly centrally planned. Michelangelo at St Peter's in Rome and Christopher Wren at St Paul's in London both proposed central plans but these were rejected by their clergy. Thus although longitudinal 'basilican' plans predominated in the west for over 1,000 years, the Benedictines at Leyland were returning to ancient precedent. With this they combined modern architectural techniques.

The new church was built in 1962–64 to the design of a Polish architect, Jerzy Faczynski, working for the firm of Weightman and Bullen, which did much work for the Roman Catholic archdiocese of Liverpool. A little earlier Frederick Gibberd had won the competition to design the archdiocese's new cathedral, for which a central plan had been prescribed by the archbishop. There are marked similarities in plan and detail between the cathedral and the Leyland church.

St Mary's is a round church constructed from brick and concrete. A radially folded roof joins the upper walls in zig-zag gables. There is a detached open framework campanile of central posts higher than the church. The building is approached by broad steps to a projecting vestibule with a canopy, below which there is a mosaic of the Last Judgement. It is rather like medieval 'doom paintings' above chancel arches which showed the saved and the damned on either of the triumphant figure of Christ.

The vestibule leads into a wide ambulatory passage that encircles the whole interior. It has its own roof lower than the body of the church, from which it is separated by a ring of forked concrete pillars. From the ambulatory the floor of the church slopes down slightly to the centre and the altar so that from all the circular benches there is a clear view of the latter. The overall effect is that of a covered arena.

The church is lit by clear glass in the ring of gables and by a small lantern above the altar. The glass that dominates the interior, however, is the remarkable set of 36 abstract stained glass windows that form the outer wall of the ambulatory in a single unified scheme. They were designed by Patrick Reyntiens, who did the principal glass, also abstract, at Liverpool Cathedral. Each window is about ten feet by six feet and set between concrete pillars, 'very beautiful in colours and shapes'. Each of the small, thick irregularly shaped pieces that together form a window is set into concrete. It is a popular form of modern glazing known as *dalles de verre* (literally 'paving stones of glass'). Dark blue colours predominate with some greens and violets. An isolated bright red appears in a few windows.

For services involving smaller congregations and for individual prayer and meditation there are a number of attractively designed side-chapels.

The artwork throughout the church is, as would be expected, of a much higher quality than that in early twentieth-century Catholic churches elsewhere. The Liverpool sculptor Arthur Dooley created a set of bronze Stations of the Cross, which are arranged on the pillars around the ambulatory. Other distinguished artists were commissioned to make statues in wood and metal, tapestries and lettering.

In a competition in 2013 organised by the National Churches Trust to find the best ten places of Christian worship built in Britain after 1953 St Mary's was awarded second place.

Many parish churches, Roman Catholic, Anglican and Free Church have since followed in the architectural footsteps of Leyland, their architects developing a large number of variations on the central plan which clearly satisfies the modern desire for services involving a closer relationship between ministers and people, between altar and pew.

Despite a decline in church attendance Christians have followed the example of their predecessors in other ages in commissioning the best architects and artists to build and beautify for the worship of God and the raising of the human spirit.

HOW TO SUPPORT
THE NATIONAL CHURCHES TRUST

MANY OF THE UK'S HISTORIC churches are fighting a battle against the ravages of time. We need to make sure they get the help they need to remain open and at the heart of the local communities for which they were built and so continue to play an integral part in all our lives.

The National Churches Trust (formerly the Historic Churches Preservation Trust) relies on the generosity of our supporters to fund our work. In 2019 we awarded grants to nearly 200 churches and chapels, and we supported many, many more.

There are many different ways in which you can support us.

BECOME A FRIEND

Thanks to the help of our Friends, we are able to fund urgent repairs to thousands of churches across the UK. By joining us today, you can help us to do even more. Not only will your support make a vital difference to our work, but you will also enjoy a range of benefits including:

- Invitations to our Friends events
- A subscription to our bi-annual Friends Newsletters and monthly Friends E-newsletters
- A complimentary copy of our Annual Review
- Special Friends offers

You can join online for just £30 a year at **www.nationalchurchestrust.org/friends** or post a cheque for £35 to the address below.

LEAVE A GIFT IN YOUR WILL

By leaving a gift in your Will to the National Churches Trust you can help us restore churches in every sense of the word. A gift of just 1% of your estate will help to guarantee that our nation's rich heritage of churches and chapels will survive for many more years to come.

If you would like more information on leaving a gift in your Will or adding a codicil, please visit our website **www.nationalchurchestrust.org/legacy**, contact us on **020 7222 0605** or email Claire Walker, Chief Executive, at **claire.walker@nationalchurchestrust.org** – there is no obligation and we would be delighted to help you further.

MAKE A DONATION

You can make a donation online at **www.nationalchurchestrust.org/donate** Our churches, chapels and meeting houses are a unique part of our national story. With your help we can do more to ensure their survival for the benefit of future generations. Thank you.

CONTACT US AT:

The National Churches Trust,
7 Tufton Street,
London   SW1P 3QB
020 7222 0605
info@nationalchurchestrust.org
www.nationalchurchestrust.org
Registered Charity Number 1119845

Opposite top: There is an ambulatory all around the back of the church. Its 36 abstract stained glass windows are a notable feature of the interior.

Opposite bottom: Two of the ambulatory panels show that predominantly blue colours were used throughout.

Right: Michael Palin, 'an agnostic with doubts', is one of the National Churches Trust's Vice Presidents. © John Swannell

Repair work at the following churches and chapels featured in this book has been supported by the National Churches Trust and the Historic Churches Preservation Trust.

LOCATION	DEDICATION
Kilpeck, Herefordshire	St Mary and St David
Tewkesbury, Gloucestershire	The Abbey Church of St Mary
Selby, North Yorkshire	The Abbey Church of our Lord, St Mary and St Germain
West Walton, Norfolk	St Mary
Beverley, East Yorkshire	Beverley Minster
Ripple, Worcestershire	St Mary
Blythburgh, Suffolk	Holy Trinity
Cullomptom, Devon	St Andrew
Fotheringhay, Northamptonshire	St Mary and All Saints
Exton, Leicestershire	St Peter and St Paul
City of London	St Stephen Walbrook
Mereworth, Kent	St Lawrence
Great Witley, Worcestershire	St Michael and All Angels
Well, Lincolnshire	St Margaret
Shobdon, Herefordshire	St John the Evangelist
Whitby, North Yorkshire	St Mary
Come-to-Good, Cornwall	The Quaker Meeting House
St Austell, Cornwall	Methodist Chapel of St John
Sefton Park, Liverpool, Lancashire	St Agnes
Brampton, Cumbria	St Martin

GOOD INVESTMENT

For people who love church buildings